THE COLD WIND AND THE WARM

THE

Cold Wind

AND THE

Warm

A Play by S. N. BEHRMAN

(Suggested by his *New Yorker* series
and book *The Worcester Account*)

Random House  New York

For

ROBERT WHITEHEAD

THE COLD WIND AND THE WARM *was first presented by The Producers Theatre and Robert Whitehead at the Morosco Theatre, New York City, on December 8, 1958, with the following cast:*

(IN ORDER OF APPEARANCE)

TOBEY	Timmy Everett
WILLIE	Eli Wallach
JIM NIGHTINGALE	Vincent Gardenia
DAN	Sidney Armus
IDA	Maureen Stapleton
REN	Jada Rowland
MYRA	Carol Grace
AARON	Peter Trytler
RAPPAPORT	Sig Arno
MR. SACHER (FATHER)	Morris Carnovsky
LEAH	Suzanne Pleshette
NORBERT MANDEL	Sanford Meisner

Directed by Harold Clurman
Settings by Boris Aronson
Costumes by Motley
Lighting by Feder

Act One

Worcester, Massachusetts, summer 1908, early evening.

Act Two

Scene 1. Sunday afternoon, one and a half years later.

Scene 2. Late afternoon the next day.

Scene 3. A month later.

Scene 4. Several days later.

Act Three

New York City, five years later.

Scene 1. Tobey's and Willie's room. Ida's living room.

Scene 2. Next evening.

Scene 3. Immediately following.

Scene 4. Some time later—Worcester.

ACT ONE

ACT ONE

As the curtain rises, the stage is dark. We hear TOBEY's *voice. He is nearing sixty, and the voice comes from his meditation on a vanished past and particularly on the enigma of a lost but still-abiding friendship of his youth. Through the dissolving darkness we hear a lovely, plaintive melody: the oboe passage from the second movement of Handel's* Water Music.

TOBEY's VOICE   I find as I grow older that I keep going back to my friendship with Willie—when we were young and happy and living in Worcester, Massachusetts, in the early years of the century. Willie was always preoccupied with mystery—the mystery of life—the mystery of death. He used to illuminate all my childish problems for me. But he left me an inheritance of the greatest mystery of all: why he killed himself, why he felt he had to do it. What were the steep dark walls in Willie's mind that converged on him to destroy him? I don't know. What I do know, as I look back on my relationship with him— and on his relationships with others—was that he was the most life-giving person I have ever known. I remember still the first mysteries I brought him to solve: the mystery of infinity, the mystery of the True Name of the Lord. Did Willie, at the end, ponder these mysteries? Had he sought the True Name? Did he, I wonder, come too close? I don't know. I shall never know. I can only tell what I can remember.

> (*While* TOBEY's *meditation is going on, we gradually light up to the scene of the play: an early evening in the summer of 1908, in Worcester, Massachusetts. Then we see* WILLIE LAVIN *and* TOBEY *standing at the foot of the hill.* WILLIE *is a young man of twenty,* TOBEY *is a boy of*

3

twelve, wearing glasses and carrying a strapped bag of school books. They are deep in talk. We can dimly see DR. JIM NIGHTINGALE *in his office on the other side of the stage, engrossed in practicing his oboe. He continues playing the oboe passage from Handel)*

TOBEY   Willie, my father is always telling me not to think about things.

WILLIE   What things?

TOBEY   All sorts of things.

WILLIE   For example?
 (TOBEY *stops, in the grip of the mystery*)

TOBEY   Now, Willie . . . look . . .

WILLIE   (*Very sympathetic*)   Yes, Tobey?

TOBEY   We're standing here, aren't we—at the corner of Exchange and Green?

WILLIE   Precisely.

TOBEY   Above us is the sky. Right?

WILLIE   Right.

TOBEY   Now above that sky—let's say a million miles away—there's another sky.

WILLIE   I'll grant that.

TOBEY Let's say there are a million skies beyond that sky. A trillion. All right?

WILLIE I'm with you, Tobey—at the trillionth sky.

TOBEY (*His voice rising in triumph*) Well, what's beyond the *last* sky? There *must* be an end to it someplace. At night I build a big wall to end it. But what's beyond the wall?

WILLIE Infinity.

TOBEY (*Clinches it*) That's what Father says I mustn't think about!

WILLIE (*As they walk down the street*) I disagree with your father. It's a problem—like other problems. It can be analyzed. Resolved into its component parts.

TOBEY (*With sublime confidence in* WILLIE) I *knew* you'd have some ideas about it, Willie! You're a scientist! You know everything.
   (*The sound of the oboe captures them*)

WILLIE Dr. Jim Nightingale practicing his oboe. Let's look in on him. What else does your father tell you not to think about?

TOBEY It seems that the Lord has many names but no one knows the *True* Name. He tells me not to try to find out the True Name.

WILLIE Why not?

TOBEY Because my father says that those who come close to it are destroyed. But infinity does bother me.

WILLIE (*Musing aloud*) Perhaps if you solved infinity you'd find out the True Name of the Lord also. Perhaps there's only one mystery—the key to everything—and you'd get it in one blinding flash—

TOBEY Father says not to think of those things at all—

WILLIE Your father and I are always arguing about that. I say there must be no limits to inquiry. *He* says—
  (*But by this time they are at* DR. JIM NIGHTINGALE'S *door.* WILLIE *presses the bell and smiles at* TOBEY. *We see the outer room of* DR. JIM NIGHTINGALE'S *office. It is very shabby, with a dilapidated, sagging horsehair sofa.* DR. NIGHTINGALE, *a rusty dressed, stocky little man of about forty, with vivacious dark eyes and dark skin, cherry-cheeked, is standing before a music stand, tootling on his oboe with complete absorption. The doorbell rings. With tremendous annoyance the doctor puts down his oboe and opens the front door. When he sees* WILLIE *and* TOBEY, *his annoyance changes to pleasure*)

JIM Come in! (*Opens the door*) Oh, you two! Delighted. I was scared to death it was a patient.

WILLIE We heard the oboe. Knew you weren't busy.

JIM (*With a gesture toward the sofa*) Sit ye doon. I'd rather be interrupted when I *am* busy. Still, I'm always glad to see *you*, Willie.
  (WILLIE *sits on a stool.* TOBEY *sits on the sofa*)

TOBEY (*Shyly*) It's a sad sound, the oboe.

JIM (*Points to music on stand*) Handel's *Water Music*—Ought to hear my teacher play it. First oboeist of the Boston Symphony.

TOBEY I'd like to be a pianist.

JIM Why don't you?

TOBEY No piano in the house.

JIM (*Takes an obstetrical manual from a shelf*) Here! Amuse yourself with this.

WILLIE (*Curious*) What's that?

JIM (*Winks at* WILLIE) Manual of obstetrics. The kids come in here and devour the illustrations.

TOBEY (*Rises, moves back. Blushing furiously*) No, thanks.

JIM (*Urging it on him*) Come on—nothing wrong with it. It's science. Maybe you'll be a gynecologist. Easier than being a pianist . . .

TOBEY (*Hideously embarrassed*) No, thanks.

WILLIE Quit it, Jim. You're embarrassing him.

JIM What's embarrassing about the facts of life? (*But he gives up as he sees* TOBEY'*s averted face, and throws the book on the sofa. He picks up a magazine instead and gives that to* TOBEY) Well, here's "Puck." You can look at the funny pictures . . . (TOBEY *grabs it, happy to absorb himself in "Puck."* JIM *turns to* WILLIE) Well, Willie, how're you getting on at W.P.I.? How's the chemistry? What are you on?

7

WILLIE Knee-deep in colloids.

JIM Who've you got?

WILLIE Professor Jackson.

JIM Oh, he's good, Professor Jackson. He comes in here. I have good talks with Jackson. Wish to hell I'd stuck to science.

WILLIE (*Comforts him*) Medicine's science.

JIM Medicine may be science, but practicing medicine isn't. Good God—the women who come in here with their imaginary pains—they're bored with their husbands so they— By the way, Tobey?

TOBEY (*Looks up from "Puck"*) Yes, Dr. Nightingale?

JIM How's your mother?

TOBEY She's gone to New York to see Professor Jacobi.

JIM I know that. When's she coming home?

TOBEY I don't know.

JIM All right, kid. (TOBEY *goes back to "Puck."* JIM *turns to* WILLIE) They haven't got the money to rent a piano for the kid, but to send his mother to New York . . .

WILLIE Well, when it's a question of health . . .

8

JIM She's got chronic asthma. I've done everything I can for her. But they send her to New York to see Professor Jacobi! What a practice I have! (*Points to his oboe*) Well, that little instrument . . . that little tube of wood and brass . . . saves my life. (*The telephone in his inside office rings*) Damn that telephone! Well, let it ring!

TOBEY (*Rises, shocked*) But maybe somebody is dying!

JIM (*Amused by* TOBEY's *concern*) All right, kid.
(JIM *goes inside to take the call*)

TOBEY He must be the busiest doctor in Worcester and yet he finds the time for . . .
(*He points to the music stand*)

WILLIE Oh, Jim Nightingale's quite a character. With all his talk and cynicism he's very good-hearted.

TOBEY (*Sits on sofa*) No one ever pays him. I heard my father offer to pay him something. He always says no hurry. And he goes twice a week to Boston for music lessons. (*Dreaming for a moment*) If there's one thing in the world I'd like to do . . .

WILLIE What?

TOBEY Play the piano.

WILLIE Well—why not?

TOBEY No piano. No teacher.

WILLIE (*Musing*) Pianos exist. Teachers exist. They are procurable.

9

TOBEY   I don't see how.

WILLIE (*Cracks his knuckles*)   Let me consider this problem. Let me resolve it into its component parts.

TOBEY   Willie? What's a gynecologist?
  (WILLIE *is stumped for a moment—he is saved the embarrassment of definition by* JIM's *return*)

JIM (*Cheerfully*)   Well, the kid was right . . . somebody *is* dying!
  (*He picks up his oboe*)

TOBEY (*Aghast*)   Well—aren't you going to do something?

JIM   Oh, don't worry, it isn't going to happen tonight. (*To* WILLIE, *as he puts the oboe down*) Diabetes.

WILLIE (*Casually*)   Who?

JIM (*Equally casually*)   Your friend Dan Eisner. There! I violated a professional oath. Hippocrates will blackball me at his club.

WILLIE (*Stunned*)   Dan Eisner!

JIM   Don't say anything. (*Wants to change the subject*) Willie, speaking of colloids and Professor Jackson—

WILLIE (*Rises*)   But Dan Eisner! It's not possible!

JIM   Why? Is he immortal?

WILLIE (*Stupidly*)   But he's going to be married!

10

JIM (*Flatly*)   Marriage is no cure for diabetes!

WILLIE   But, Jim—does Dan know it—have you told him?

JIM   I've told him what he's got. Let him draw his own conclusions. He's not an idiot.

WILLIE   Then how can he contemplate—how can he—

JIM   He doesn't trust me, I guess. Maybe he'll see Professor Jacobi.

WILLIE   But Myra—does she know?

JIM   If he's told her, she knows. If he hasn't, she doesn't. None of my business.

WILLIE   But if it's true—then Myra—

JIM   In three or four years she'll be a beautiful widow. That's a good kind of widow to be! (*He sees that* WILLIE *has been tremendously affected by the news about* DAN EISNER) Oh, I forgot. You're in love with Myra yourself. Well, bide your time, Willie . . .
   (TOBEY, *aware of* WILLIE's *tension, looks up from his magazine.* WILLIE *is under a terrific strain and very much annoyed with* JIM *for dragging his emotional life into the open, especially in front of* TOBEY, *to whom he is a hero. He turns to go*)

WILLIE   Well, Tobey, time to move on, I guess.
   (TOBEY *gets up, at the ready*)

JIM (*Rises*) What about dinner? I'll treat you both at Putnam and Thurston's.

WILLIE No, thank you, Jim. We've eaten.

JIM Sorry if what I told you . . .

WILLIE (*Anything to get off that subject*) That sofa is pretty dilapidated, Jim. Been here since I can remember. Can't you afford a new sofa?

JIM Wouldn't give up that sofa for anything!

WILLIE Certainly sags in the middle.

JIM Symbol of conquest! I've been treating bored wives on that sofa for twenty years!

WILLIE (*Shushes him, whispers*) Please, not in front of the boy! (*To* TOBEY) Come on, Tobey.
(TOBEY *is beside him;* JIM *walks them to the door*)

JIM (*To* TOBEY, *at the door*) Come in any time—my medical library is at your disposal. (*He tousles* TOBEY's *head. To* WILLIE) You too, Willie—any time—we'll talk chemistry.

WILLIE (*Can't wait to be off*) Sure.

TOBEY Good-bye, Dr. Nightingale. Thank you.

JIM Good-bye, kid.

WILLIE So long, Jim.
(*The moment they go* JIM *is back at the music stand and*

12

playing Handel's Water Music. *This music carries us over to the first part of the next scene. Once they are outside,* WILLIE *and* TOBEY *start walking down the street)*

TOBEY You didn't answer my question—what's a gynecologist?
>   (DAN EISNER, *his manner defiantly athletic, walks by on his way to* JIM's *office)*

WILLIE Hello, Dan—
>   (DAN *waves to them, goes on to ring the doctor's doorbell)*

TOBEY (*Full of wonder*) But, Willie! How can Dan be dying? His tie, Willie—his collar and tie . . .

WILLIE (*Very abstracted by* JIM's *devastating revelation. To* TOBEY, *mechanically*) What's his tie got to do with it?

TOBEY (*Bubbles eagerly*) Just like the posters of John Drew—you've seen them, Willie? A high stiff collar—with straight lines—and his tie, knotted so nice between them—
>   (*His voice trails off in awe and wonder*)

WILLIE I still don't see . . .

TOBEY I mean—if he's dying—how can he take so much trouble with his tie?

WILLIE Maybe he doesn't believe it. (WILLIE *and* TOBEY *walk on through the leafy summer evening—full of promise—of that evening, of the next day, of the veiled funnel of the future. The lights dim down and come up, revealing the*

*façade of 31 Providence Street. The first and second floor
piazzas are stage right. The porch and stoop are left of center.*
WILLIE *and* TOBEY *enter stage right, walking up the hill*) It
could be done, you know.

TOBEY   What?

WILLIE   Piano lessons.

TOBEY   But who'd pay for it?

WILLIE   I would. I have great faith in your future.

TOBEY   All your friends wonder why you spend so much time
with me.

WILLIE   Can't discuss abstract questions with my friends. Nice
fellows, but they're a bit excessively down to earth.

TOBEY   I'm lucky to have a friend like you.

WILLIE   It's a natural affinity between sympathetic tempera-
ments.
   (*He smiles at* TOBEY. TOBEY *glows. By this time they
   have reached the stoop in front of the house. They sit
   down on it*)

TOBEY (*Suddenly*)   You know what I think Dan should do...

WILLIE   That's mental telepathy. I was thinking about Dan
too...

TOBEY   I know just what he should do.

14

WILLIE   About Myra you mean?

TOBEY   No—about the angel. The Dark Angel. The Angel of
Death. Dan should do what I do. He should hold on tight—
to the bedposts. Like this.
   (*He illustrates, stretching his arms up and holding on to
   the railing of the steps on which they are sitting, in a
   kind of lopsided crucifixion*)

WILLIE   (*Humors him*)   You don't think the Dark Angel
might be stronger?

TOBEY   No. You can outfight him if you hold on fast enough.
He comes at night. He's always at our house, you know,
Willie—to take my mother. Every night Father says his night
prayer, about those four good angels . . . and I have confidence in them, so I fall asleep. But then I wake up—and he's
standing there, the Dark One, grabbing at me, to take me
away . . .

WILLIE   (*Fascinated*)   What's he look like?

TOBEY   He hasn't got any face—yet he looks at you—with *something*. He's not angry or anything—he just wants to take you.

WILLIE   And you don't let him?

TOBEY   No. I hold on to the bedposts. The more he tugs, the
more I hold on. That's what Mother should do and that's
what Dan should do!

WILLIE   Have you told your mother?

TOBEY When she has one of her attacks—I can't—her hands look so weak . . . her hands, Willie . . .

WILLIE (*Quietly*) Yes, Tobey?

TOBEY Her hands look as if they already belonged to the Dark One.

WILLIE (*After a moment*) I think maybe, Tobey . . . I think maybe you read too much.
> (IDA *comes out on piazza, anxiously looking up and down Providence Street. She is expecting someone.* IDA *is about forty, with large clear, candid blue eyes—she has the look of one of Holbein's matrons*)

TOBEY (*Calling up to her*) Hello, Aunt Ida.

WILLIE Good evening, Aunt Ida.

IDA Tobey—Willie—what you two have to talk about all the time I don't know, but any minute I'm expecting Leah from Fitchburg.

WILLIE Oh, I know. The entire hill is expecting Leah from Fitchburg.

IDA She'll be on the Providence Street car. Wait till you see her, Willie, you'll right away melt.

WILLIE Why do you dangle this paragon in front of me, Ida? You're marrying her off to somebody else, aren't you?

IDA To a very rich millionaire from Atlanta.

WILLIE   Why should I melt in vain?

TOBEY   Why doesn't he go right to Fitchburg? Why does he have to come here?

IDA   Because he's very high-tone, the furrier from Atlanta, and Fitchburg is no place to meet a bride.

TOBEY   What's wrong with Fitchburg?

IDA   When your uncle—may he rest in peace—married me he took me for a honeymoon to Fitchburg on the streetcar. It spoiled the whole honeymoon. So be sure, Willie, and bring her up the moment she gets here. (IDA *goes inside. The lights come up, right, as part of the façade of the building is flown off, revealing* IDA's *parlor.* REN, *her daughter, an attractive girl of fifteen, is lying on the sofa.* REN *is absorbed in* The Ancient Mariner. *A large framed photograph of* IDA's *father, the Ramov, hangs on the wall: a venerable man with a full white beard, Moses with spectacles.* IDA *looks around her domain with satisfaction*) It looks nice everything, you think so, Ren? She will like it, Leah from Fitchburg. Atlanta will like it? You like it, Ren?

REN   (*Without looking up from* The Ancient Mariner)   Fine.

IDA   (*Mild reproval*)   Why do you say fine when you don't even look? Maybe you will go up the hill to Lover's Lane and bring back some flowers?

REN   I'm trying to do my homework!

IDA   So you'll be a schoolteacher two weeks later!

17

REN (*With scorn*) I have a feeling that this furrier is nowhere near as high-tone as you think he is!

IDA What are you talking, Ren? So rich is the furrier that his apartment is furnished by an interior man. I showed you his picture, Ren?
> (*She rummages in a drawer of a desk, takes out a photograph and shows it to the inattentive* REN)

REN (*Glances at the furrier's picture, disdainful*) Looks more like a trapper than a furrier!

IDA (*Studying the photograph with detachment*) Handsome he is, but he has no neck.

REN Why was Pa so anxious about Leah?

IDA Before he went into the real estate your father used to peddle around Fitchburg. Leah's mother ran there a restaurant, and Poppa used to go there. Before she died she begged him, "Please, Harry, ask your wife she should find for Leah!"

REN Well, that's your specialty. Finding! Why didn't you?

IDA To find for Leah I didn't trust myself, so I went to a professional. I went to Rappaport, the matchmaker from Boston. So he found Atlanta. Leah's picture he sent to Atlanta. Atlanta's picture he sent to Leah.

REN (*In a flare up of rebellion*) Oh, Ma. It's so boring here. Why don't we go to New York to live?

IDA Of this I am thinking. Already I wrote to my father, the Ramov.

REN   Well, what did he say?

IDA   He said wait till you get through high school. Then you can go to City College in New York!

REN   (*Dramatically*)   A whole year! It's ETERNITY!

IDA   A whole year goes by like five minutes!

REN   Maybe for you. Not for me. Besides, I don't think that's the real reason . . .

IDA   So what is?

REN   (*Accusingly*)   You're in love with Mr. Mandel, the land-lord—that's why!

IDA   I am not in love till I find out if I am loved back!

REN   Well, I wish you'd hurry up and find out!

IDA   I have to go into the kitchen to make for Leah a snack.
      (IDA *goes into kitchen.* REN *stretches out on the sofa again, props* The Ancient Mariner *in front of her and goes on reading. The lights dim down and come up on the stoop. We hear the sound of the passing streetcar*)

TOBEY   I wonder if Leah is on this one?

WILLIE   The conductor didn't stop.

TOBEY   I love the sound of the streetcar. Especially at night. Don't you? I hear it go by when I'm in bed. I think of the people inside. I go along with them, inside the car, to the

top of the hill. It stops at Lover's Lane. But I don't let it stop.
I keep it going. Beyond Lover's Lane, down the other side,
and on and on . . . all round the world—till it comes to Main
and Pleasant again. When I hear it next time, it's been all
around the world. It must be wonderful to travel. Do you
think I'll ever travel?

WILLIE   Why not?
>(MYRA, *a lovely blond girl, and* AARON, *an intensely in-*
>*trospective young man, come down the hill.* MYRA *comes*
>*to* WILLIE, *bubbling and reproachful.* AARON *stands by,*
>*smoldering and sullen*)

MYRA   Willie!

WILLIE   Good evening, Myra. Hello, Aaron.

AARON   Hello.

MYRA   I hate you, Willie! I just hate you. You never come to
see me any more. Why, I haven't see you in ages!

WILLIE   Well, you are betrothed to another. You're practically
a married woman.

MYRA   That's the awful thing about being engaged. Everybody
drops you!

WILLIE   (*Virtuously*)   They should.

MYRA   (*With sudden apprehension of loneliness*)   Will it be
like that *after* I'm married? Will no one come to see me? Oh
gee, that would be awful.

20

WILLIE You're supposed to "cleave unto" your husband. That's what the service says. You're gonna have to cleave—all the time—

MYRA But I just love having boys around who adore me and I love to adore them back. That's all the fun—flirting—(*She giggles*) With me flirting is almost everything. If I flirt with anybody that means I'm a little bit in love with them . . .

WILLIE (*With some bitterness*) Well, you've got Aaron, haven't you—while you're waiting to marry his older brother.

MYRA But I love to flirt with *you,* Willie . . .

AARON Please, Myra. I thought you wanted to read my poem.

MYRA I'm just dying to read it. (*To* WILLIE) Aaron's written a poem. It's dedicated to me. He dedicates all his poems to me!

WILLIE When is the happy event to take place?

MYRA (*Archly*) That's for me to know and for you to find out!

WILLIE Oh, come on! What's the big secret?

MYRA (*Mysteriously*) We may elope!

WILLIE When?

MYRA What's the point of eloping if I tell you when . . .

AARON (*Miserable*) Myra! Do you want to hear my poem or don't you?

MYRA (*Takes his arm*) I'm dying to read it, Aaron. (*She starts up stoop steps with* AARON. *To* WILLIE) Don't forget me entirely, Willie—please . . .
       (MYRA *and* AARON *disappear through the main doorway of the house*)

TOBEY Is Aaron in love with Myra too?

WILLIE She drives him crazy. Cradle snatching. Dan's younger brother, too. She shouldn't have.

TOBEY Is *everybody* in love with Myra? (WILLIE *doesn't answer*) Are you really in love with her, Willie? (WILLIE *still doesn't speak*) She's pretty. (*As* WILLIE *still says nothing*) Aunt Ida's always arranging for people to get married. Is she arranging for Dan and Myra to get married?

WILLIE No. Your Aunt Ida had nothing to do with that. That was spontaneous combustion.

TOBEY What's that?

WILLIE (*A moment.* WILLIE *is in a brown study, thinking about the news he has had from* JIM) Tobey? I'm in something of a dilemma. (*Doesn't bother to explain*) I think your father could help me. He's the only one I could think of. Is he home?

TOBEY Well, he might be. But on Thursday nights he stays late at the grocery.

WILLIE   Let's go up and see.

(*We see them go up the stoop steps, through the main doorway of house and into* TOBEY's *tenement, which is directly behind porch and continues left of it. Light comes up, revealing the parlor of* TOBEY's *father's tenement. It is chiefly furnished with great Talmudic tomes.* TOBEY *and* WILLIE *sit down at a table.* WILLIE *sees two books, both open, which* TOBEY *has been reading. He picks one up, looking at it as* TOBEY *goes to the bedroom door, calling for his father. There is no answer. He comes back*)

TOBEY   Father's not home yet.

WILLIE   There's a book I've been meaning to give you that I think you'll find very interesting. What are you reading now, Tobey?

TOBEY   *Hamlet* and Horatio Alger.

WILLIE   *Hamlet* is good. What a vocabulary that man had!

TOBEY   He certainly did!

WILLIE   (*Rises. Declaiming*)   "This majestical roof, look you, this brave o'erhanging firmament fretted with golden fire . . ." (*Pauses to give* TOBEY *a chance*)   How does it go from there?

TOBEY   "What a piece of work is man! How noble in reason! How infinite in faculty . . ."

WILLIE   (*Muses*)   "How infinite in faculty!" That's great. You won't find stuff like that in Alger.

TOBEY   What's the book you've got for me?

WILLIE   *Looking Backward,* by Edward Bellamy. Paradoxically enough, it's all about the future. Utopia.

TOBEY   (*Lit up with enthusiasm*)   Oh, I'd love to read it.

WILLIE   I'll run up the hill and get it for you now.

TOBEY   I'll come with you.

WILLIE   (*Pushes strapped school books toward* TOBEY)   No, you stay here and do your homework. I'll be right back.
   (WILLIE *exits.* TOBEY *starts to unstrap his school books, but then the Alger catches his eye. He picks it up, reads aloud*)

TOBEY   *From Canal Boy to President.*
   (*He puts the school books away and settles for the Alger. As he settles down absorbed, the lights dim. We see* WILLIE *go down to the stoop. He bumps into* RAPPAPORT. RAPPAPORT *is a wispy little man dressed with seedy professional elegance. He carries a small nosegay*)

RAPPAPORT   I beg your pardon, sir.

WILLIE   Well, I bumped into you.

RAPPAPORT   Oh, don't mention it! Do you happen to know where Mrs. Feinberg resides?

WILLIE   (*Points*)   In there on the left.

RAPPAPORT   I'm much obliged to you.

WILLIE Are you the gentleman from Atlanta?

RAPPAPORT No, Rappaport from Boston.
  (*He goes into the house and knocks on* IDA's *door.* WILLIE
  goes on. IDA's *tenement lights up*)

REN (*Jumps up. Calls to* IDA) Ma, Leah from Fitchburg's here.
  (IDA *runs in from kitchen, opens the door, aquiver with
  anticipation. But it is* RAPPAPORT *from Boston*)

RAPPAPORT (*With a gallant bow. Presenting his bouquet*)
  Good evening, Mrs. Feinberg. I find you in good health, I
  hope.

IDA (*All in one breath*) You too. This is my daughter Ren.
  She studies. Mr. Rappaport, the matchmaker from Boston.
  (REN *nods*)

RAPPAPORT (*Outdoes himself with* REN) To meet the daughter
  of Mrs. Feinberg and the grand-daughter of the Ramov is a
  double pleasure, I assure you.

IDA For her maybe when the time comes you'll find.

RAPPAPORT (*Tartuffe*) Where does there breathe anyone so
  worthy?

REN (*To* RAPPAPORT) Whoever he is, I hope he breathes in
  New York!

IDA (*Dismisses her*) Go, darling, study in the kitchen. (REN
  picks up her homework and goes. IDA *confronts* RAPPAPORT)
  So, Rappaport, what is? Everything is settled, yes? Tomorrow you bring the furrier from Atlanta. So he'll see the fur-

rier Leah has connections he shouldn't be ashamed. In the house of the daughter of the Ramov everybody *can't* come.

RAPPAPORT (*Begins to sprinkle cold water*)   Your father is the most famous rabbi in the world. So famous is he that all over the world he is known by his initials . . . R-A-M-O-V. Ramov. So for me it is an honor. But for the furrier from Atlanta it is not such an honor.

IDA (*Bridles*)   What is with the furrier that it isn't an honor?

RAPPAPORT   He is such a coarse fellow the furrier that, would you believe it Mrs. Feinberg, when I wrote him you are the daughter of the Ramov, he wrote me back: "And who is the Ramov?" Can you imagine such a coarse fellow?

IDA   A coarse fellow he is all of a sudden? Last time you told me he's the Prince from Wales. Stop beating, Rappaport. What time do you come tomorrow with the furrier? (RAPPA-PORT *starts coughing to gain time*) This coughing I don't like, Rappaport. (RAPPAPORT's *cough gets worse*) This cough is not from a cold and it is not from a tickle. This cough is from not answering. With Leah from Fitchburg you wrote me it's fixed. *Is* it fixed or are you coughing yourself out of the fix?

RAPPAPORT (*No way out, he masters his cough*)   With the fur-rier you should forgive me, Mrs. Feinberg, I have made a little mistake, though my fault it wasn't. An act of God took place.

IDA (*Without emotion*)   He died the furrier?

RAPPAPORT   No, the furrier, thanks God, is alive.

IDA   Then what mistake?

RAPPAPORT   Mrs. Feinberg, I have to explain you.
(*He starts coughing again*)

IDA   (*Very severe*)   Don't begin again with that coughing, Rappaport. Explain!

RAPPAPORT   With you, Mrs. Feinberg, matchmaking is a hobby. You don't make from it. But hobbies, *I* can't afford. From matchmaking I have to make a living, Mrs. Feinberg.

IDA   He won't pay you your commission, that stingy furrier?

RAPPAPORT   He pays.

IDA   So what are you grabbling me?

RAPPAPORT   (*In extremis*)   Pay he will, but not for Leah.

IDA   But with Leah—yourself you told me—when you sent the furrier Leah's picture—he right away melted.

RAPPAPORT   Of that, Mrs. Feinberg, there can be no doubt.

IDA   So give me direct!

RAPPAPORT   With Leah's picture—don't forget I have to make a living, Mrs. Feinberg—I sent along another picture to make smaller the risk.

IDA   (*Withering*)   Who did you send?

RAPPAPORT   Goldie from Revere Beach.

IDA (*Full of scorn*) Goldie from Revere Beach, then I'm not worried! To Goldie I brought myself three men. They all ran away. Goldie from Revere Beach speaks with a palate. With Goldie you can't tell whether she is saying yes or no.

RAPPAPORT To the furrier she said yes.

IDA (*Stunned*) What are you telling, Rappaport?

RAPPAPORT How should I know Goldie's mother will take it in her head to travel with Goldie to Atlanta? Moreandover, from the furrier Goldie's mother bought Goldie a fur coat—mink. Here mink, there mink, all mink.

IDA (*With mounting fury*) You wrote me it's fixed.

RAPPAPORT (*With calculated sadness*) It is. For Goldie.
    (*A silence.* IDA's *eyes flash.* RAPPAPORT *is quite nervous*)

IDA (*Murderously quiet, as she advances on him. He rises and slithers away from her*) You know what I could do to you, Rappaport, and with pleasure—I could tear you from each limb!

RAPPAPORT (*Pitiful*) I beg you, Mrs. Feinberg, be a little bit reasonable. How could I tell that Goldie's mother . . . ?

IDA (*Shouts*) Why did you have to send that other picture?

RAPPAPORT (*Pharisaical*) That was my little mistake. Who isn't entitled to a little mistake?

IDA (*Majestic, with great dignity, no anger*) Rappaport! That you are a nudnick I always knew. Only now I find out that besides being a nudnick you are also—do you hear me Rappaport?—a no-good-Benedict-the-traitor!

RAPPAPORT   These are hard words, Mrs. Feinberg.

IDA   It is a strict report.

RAPPAPORT   Mrs. Feinberg, I promise you if you give me from Leah another photograph . . .

IDA   You will excuse me, Rappaport, but Leah's photograph is too private for a public matchmaker that deals with crooks. And as for this furrier—to him I do—(*She picks up Atlanta's photograph*)—what I'd like to do to you, Rappaport. A neck he hasn't got or I'd break it!
   (*She tears the Atlantan's photograph to pieces and hurls them into* RAPPAPORT's *face*)

RAPPAPORT   (*Really desperate, he cannot afford to have* IDA *for an enemy*)   Mrs. Feinberg, I promise—on my late wife's memory, may she rest in peace—I promise you to make a match for Leah from Fitchburg. On my word of honor, Mrs. Feinberg, I swear you . . .

IDA   Don't swear, Rappaport, by what you haven't got.

RAPPAPORT   When you are more calm, Mrs. Feinberg, I am sure that . . .

IDA   (*Grandly*)   When I am more calm, Rappaport, I'll be sorry I didn't cripple you in the limbs. But it's good I didn't because a cripple can't walk out of the room. (*Dramatically she walks to the door and holds it open for him*) So march, Rappaport, before I get calmer!

RAPPAPORT (*Pleading*) Mrs. Feinberg!
> (*His cough returns. Cowering, but with enough presence of mind to retrieve the nosegay,* RAPPAPORT *makes an ignominious exit out the main doorway and up the hill.* REN *enters from kitchen. She looks at her mother with surprise; she has never seen her so angry*)

REN Why, Ma! What's wrong!

IDA (*Sits at desk in despair*) That dishonest crook from Atlanta, he isn't coming!

REN (*Quite indifferent*) Oh?

IDA And any minute is coming Leah. What will I tell poor Leah?

REN (*As she kisses* IDA) Don't worry, Ma. You'll think of something. You always do.
> (IDA *sits, dejected, pondering. The lights dim out on* IDA's *parlor as* TOBEY's *father comes to the stoop and goes up the steps, his eyes fixed on a newspaper. He is about sixty, still vigorous, with the look of a benevolent Saracen. As he walks into his parlor, the lights come up, revealing* TOBEY *still absorbed in Alger*)

TOBEY (*Without lifting his eyes from his book*) Hello, Father.

FATHER You're not reading in a good light, Tobey. You'll strain your eyes.

TOBEY (*With excitement*) Willie's coming to see you.

FATHER Oh.

TOBEY   Yes. He's got a dilemma.

FATHER *(Smiles faintly)*   I'm very tired. You should go to bed, too, Tobey. Go to bed, my boy.

TOBEY   When Willie comes, tell him I went to bed.

FATHER   I will.

TOBEY   Good night, Father.

FATHER   Sweet dreams.

TOBEY   You too. (TOBEY *starts toward the bedroom*) Do you think Mother will be well when she comes back?

FATHER   I pray so.

TOBEY   The minute she comes back, I'll show her what I do against the Dark Angel—I'll show her just how to hold onto the bedposts. Good night, Father.
(He goes. FATHER *starts pacing the room, saying his night prayers)*

FATHER   "And may the angel Michael be at my right hand, Gabriel at my left, before me Uriel, behind me Raphael, and over my head the divine presence of God." *(There is a knock on the door)* Come in.
(It is WILLIE. *He has* TOBEY's *book)*

WILLIE   A book for Tobey.

FATHER   You're very good to him. I have a rather hard time with him you know. He's very . . .

WILLIE Imaginative. At the moment he's got the Angel of Death on his mind. I'm going to make him cultivate a hobby.

FATHER Anything to chase these morbid ideas out of his mind.

WILLIE It's natural, you know. I read that children go through that stage . . . the fear of losing their parents— In Tobey's case, with his mother always.

FATHER Yes. I know.

WILLIE (*A moment*) There's something I'd like to speak to you about.

FATHER Yes?

WILLIE A dilemma. An ethical dilemma.

FATHER Yes.

WILLIE (*Awkwardly*) Just this afternoon—I found out something—by accident.

FATHER What?

WILLIE About Dan Eisner. He's very sick. He's got diabetes.

FATHER I am very sorry to hear that. How do you know?

WILLIE Jim Nightingale told me. It's only a question of time . . . And the thing is . . . (*He is flustered; he has difficulty getting it out*) This is what I wanted to ask *you* . . .

FATHER Yes?

WILLIE   Oughtn't I—tell Myra?

FATHER   (*Looks at him searchingly*)   With what motive, my son?

WILLIE   (*Embarrassed.* MR. SACHER *has touched a sensitive membrane*)   Why—to save Myra.

FATHER   Is this your motive? To save Myra?

WILLIE   (*Squirms*)   Whatever it is—don't you think she ought to be told?

FATHER   Is Jim Nightingale God?

WILLIE   (*With some heat*)   He's a damn good doctor!

FATHER   Can he read the future? How does he know that some cure will not be discovered? Or that Dan may not be the exception who recovers? My dear wife has been given up several times. Yet God has seen fit to spare her.

WILLIE   Jim says it's inevitable.

FATHER   Look into your soul, my boy. I know how you feel about Myra. If anyone tells Myra—it shouldn't be you.

WILLIE   (*Suddenly*)   Why don't *you* tell her?

FATHER   I'm a poor stumbling creature. I am not God. In any case, Willie—

WILLIE   Well?

FATHER You know—according to the ancient law—if Dan should die . . .

WILLIE (*Truculent*) Well?

FATHER Myra would be bound, unless released by Dan's family, to marry Dan's younger brother, Aaron, who professes to be in love with her too.

WILLIE What is that law?

FATHER It is called the levirate law. (FATHER *goes to book-shelves and hand him a book*) There's been a great deal written about it. Here is something on it—in English.
    (WILLIE *opens the book and starts to read it. The lights dim down and come up on the stoop.* MYRA, *leading* AARON *by the hand, walks out and sits on stoop*)

MYRA Isn't it much nicer here than in that hot parlor? This is better for reading your poem, isn't it? By moonlight! Like the *Moonlight Sonata*. Isn't it? You look so sad Aaron. Are you really so sad?

AARON (*Staring at her in dumb adoration and misery*) Yes. I look at you and I'm sad.

MYRA Do my looks make you sad?

AARON Yes. You're so beautiful, Myra. All the beauty of the world is in your face.

MYRA No one says the things you do, Aaron. (*She gets up, stretches her arms in the moonlight in an ecstasy of narcissism*) Shall I tell you something? I love to see in your eyes

34

that I am beautiful. Oh, Aaron! You'll always love me, won't you? Even after I'm married to Dan? Won't you? When you become a famous poet you'll dedicate your poems to me and I'll tell you everything and you'll tell me everything. We'll have no secrets from each other—

AARON (*Cuts in*) My poems are no good! (*Shows manuscript*) Look what the teacher wrote—in the margin.

MYRA (*Peers at paper, reads*) "Fine feeling. Expression . . ." (*Spells it out*) "B-A-N-A-L." Is that good or bad?

AARON It's bad.
     (AARON *stares hopelessly at his manuscript*)

MYRA What do you care what that old teacher says? The *feeling* is fine and that's the important thing. I go by *feeling*. With me everything is feeling. (AARON *is not comforted*. MYRA *rattles on*) Aaron, do you know something? We're going to New York on our honeymoon! (*She giggles rapturously*) Honeymoon! And guess where we're going to stay? Did Dan tell you? (AARON *shakes his head; with awe and delight* MYRA *tells him*) THE HOTEL ASTOR! It's on Broadway and Forty-second Street—right in the middle of *everything*! I'll be Right There! Can you imagine? I've never been farther than Framingham. I'll miss *you*, darling; I wish you were coming. Do you think Dan would think it's funny if I asked him to bring you? (*In ecstasy at every prospect— stretching out her arms to the Universe*) Oh, Aaron—Aaron!

AARON (*In misery, mumbles her name*) Oh, Myra—Myra . . .

MYRA I love everything. All the world. I love myself—and

35

everybody else. I love you, Aaron—in the most special way—
I *love* you, Aaron!

AARON   If you loved me you wouldn't—

MYRA   (*Pedantically*)   Marriage is an experience every girl
should have. You're too young to marry. Why, you're still in
college.
   (*The lights dim down and come up in* MR. SACHER'S
   room. We go back to WILLIE *and* FATHER. WILLIE *slams
   the book closed, throws it on the table*)

WILLIE   Well, it's interesting as history. Fossilized social cus-
toms. No contemporary relevance whatever. Nonsense.

FATHER   (*Rather stern*)   If you analyze it, you'll find it is not
nonsense.

WILLIE   We're living in Massachusetts in nineteen eight. We
are not living in ancient times.

FATHER   This will only bring us back to our old argument . . .
faith versus reason. You are a good boy, Willie . . . (*Smiles
at him*) though a scientist! You came to ask my advice. People who ask your advice usually want it to justify a course
they have already decided on. You have probably decided,
already, to tell Myra . . .

WILLIE   (*In self-defense*)   If I had, why wouldn't I just have
gone and done it . . . why did I come to you?

FATHER   Then all I can say is . . . look into your heart—ask
yourself why you're doing it. Is it to save Myra? Or to save

her for yourself? (*Going to* WILLIE) Go home, my son, and think.

> (*A silence.* WILLIE *cracks his knuckles. He is in a turmoil of indecision; he knows that* MR. SACHER *has probed to the truth*)

WILLIE Well—thank you, Mr. Sacher.

FATHER (*With tenderness for him*) Good night, my boy. (WILLIE *goes out.* MR. SACHER, *deeply disturbed, begins again to repeat his prayer, pacing the floor. Intoning*) "Before me Uriel, behind me Raphael, and over my head the divine presence of God."

> (*The lights dim out and come up on the stoop.* WILLIE *comes down*)

MYRA Aaron's been reading me the most beautiful poem you ever heard! "In the wild garden of my heart a funeral urn is buried." (*Suddenly* AARON *tears up his manuscript and runs away.* MYRA *runs after him, calling*) Aaron—what's the matter—Aaron!

> (*But he is gone, dashing down the hill*)

WILLIE Gueess you're not satisfied with Dan. You want his brother, too.

> (DAN *enters from the opposite side of stage. He greets* WILLIE *effusively but with condescension*)

DAN Ah, me bucko! (*He pounds* WILLIE *on the back*) Up to your old tricks, eh? Trying to get Myra to change her mind . . .

WILLIE On the contrary—I am trying to make her aware of her responsibility as a bride.

DAN (*Masterfully*) You don't have to worry about that. I'll take care of that. Got a little surprise for you, Myra. The ring. Want to see it?

MYRA (*Overcome*) Oh . . . Dan . . . (DAN *takes out jeweler's box and shows her the ring, flashing it in the moonlight. She coos with delight*) Oh, Dan! It's beautiful.

DAN (*With pride*) Three carat! (*Waves it before her tantalizingly*) Not yours yet, you know. (*He winks at* WILLIE. MYRA *giggles*) Depends on your behavior. Want to try it on? (*He gives her the ring. She puts it on*) Fits?

MYRA Perfect. Just perfect. I love it. Oh, Dan!
   (*She stares at her ringed finger with delight*)

DAN (*To* WILLIE, *as he takes the ring from* MYRA) Went to the lake this afternoon. I swam from Jerry Daley's bath house to Parker's Point in an hour and twenty minutes!

WILLIE (*Impressed*) That's going some. Do you have a boat follow you?

DAN No boat.

WILLIE That's dangerous. You might get a cramp.

DAN (*Omnipotent*) I don't get cramps! (*He stretches himself, does a circular exercise with his arms*) Never felt so well in my life. Tops! (*Postively crowing in triumph*) Tell you,

38

Willie, nothing like being engaged to put a fella in top physical condition. Recommend it. By the way, Myra—you haven't kissed me—as per usual . . .

MYRA (*Disinclined*)   Not in front of Willie!

DAN   That don't make it worse—it makes it better!
(*He kisses her. We see* TOBEY *sneak out of his bedroom and come down steps to the stoop wearing a nightshirt*)

WILLIE (*Amazed*)   Tobey! I thought you'd gone up to bed.

TOBEY   I couldn't fall asleep. I heard you talking. I got up.

DAN (*To* TOBEY)   Hello, kid.

TOBEY (*Tense with his mission*)   I came down, Dan—to tell you what to do.

DAN (*Smacks his lips*)   Just did it. Want to kiss Myra, Tobey?
(*Pushes* TOBEY *toward* MYRA) Willie's dying to. I won't let him but I'll let you . . .

TOBEY   I mean—about the Angel—

DAN   What angel?

TOBEY   The Angel of Death. I know he's after you.

WILLIE (*Horrified, tries to shush* TOBEY)   Tobey—hush—

TOBEY (*To* WILLIE)   I heard Father say—*you* mustn't do it—so *I* have to do it . . .

DAN (*Has gone ashen in rage*)   What's the damn kid babbling about?

TOBEY (*Not to be deterred*) You must hold on tight to the
bedposts . . . don't let him take your hand away . . . once
you let him . . . you'll be . . . you'll be . . .

DAN (*In a fury*) Shut up, you little . . . (*He starts to strike*
TOBEY. WILLIE *interposes, shielding* TOBEY. DAN *turns on*
WILLIE) You put him up to this, you bastard!

MYRA (*Frightened*) What does he mean? Dan . . . ?

WILLIE (*Explains to both of them*) You know with his mother
sick all the time he has these fantasies at night . . . he's
afraid he's going to lose his mother . . .

MYRA But why to Dan?

DAN (*To* WILLIE; *he is trembling with anger and with fear too*)
I won't forget this—I'll tell you that!

MYRA Dan! Is there anything wrong with you?

DAN (*Shouts*) I'm in great shape I tell you! Never felt better
in my life!

MYRA Then why are you so . . . so . . . ?

DAN (*In better control; with mechanical bravado, points to*
WILLIE) It's that jealous . . . He put the kid up to it. (*To*
WILLIE) Won't do you a bit of good, my friend. (*To* MYRA,
masterfully) You come upstairs with me. Away from these
. . . How do you like the ring? Let me see it *on* you.

MYRA (*Completely diverted, flashes the ring before her with a slow, undulating motion*) It's just beautiful. I just love it! (*She takes it from him and slips it on her finger*)

DAN (*Jumps up the stairs*) Come on, Myra.

MYRA (*Hypnotized by the ring*) They're bound to notice it, don't you think so, Willie, in the lobby of the Hotel Astor?

DAN (*From the top of the stoop*) I'm waiting for you, Myra!

MYRA Coming Dan . . .
(*She follows him; they disappear up the steps into the house. A silence for a moment between* WILLIE *and* TOBEY)

TOBEY Are you angry with me, Willie?

WILLIE No, but your father will be if he finds out you're not in bed.

TOBEY (*As he goes up on stoop and sits on the bench*) How can Myra not love you, Willie?

WILLIE (*Following him*) She manages!
(WILLIE *has taken a little bottle out of his sweater pocket, uncorked it, and he now shakes some liquid onto his hands and rubs them dry*)

TOBEY What's that?

WILLIE Alcohol. Air is full of germs. Protects the hands from germs.
(*He replaces the bottle in his sweater pocket*)

TOBEY I'll be glad when Myra gets married.

WILLIE (*Sits beside him*) Why?

TOBEY I don't know—I just feel—I don't know—I'll be glad.

WILLIE I'm going to wait for her.

TOBEY (*Shocked, scared*) You mean you're going to wait—till the Dark One takes Dan away?

WILLIE Yes.

TOBEY Gee, that's scarey.

WILLIE (*Edgy*) Why?

TOBEY I don't know. It seems . . . something funny about it.

WILLIE (*Gets up*) I know what you feel. Tell you the truth, it kind of scares me too.

TOBEY Then why do you do it?

WILLIE Myra will need me. (*A moment*) It's not for anything to happen to Dan I'm waiting. It's for Myra to be free I'll wait.

TOBEY (*Quickly*) But isn't it the same thing? (*This is unanswerable.* WILLIE *is stumped*)

WILLIE (*Finally, with a sense of guilty evasion*) You have a logical mind, Tobey!

42

TOBEY Anyway, Father says if anything happens to Dan, Aaron will have the right—

WILLIE I'd like to see them try it! I'm beginning to think you're much too preoccupied with angels. (*Sits beside him*) Might be a good idea if you cultivated an outdoor hobby.

TOBEY (*That would settle it*) Have *you* got one?

WILLIE I am beginning to think seriously about fishing.

TOBEY Why don't you?

WILLIE First I have to master the *theory* of fishing. There's a considerable literature, you know, on fishing—different methods, different techniques.

TOBEY Allie Seidenberg just fishes.

WILLIE Well, he's just an empiricist.

TOBEY What's an empiricist?

WILLIE I'll explain that to you on one of our walks. (*Smiles at* TOBEY) The peripatetic method.

TOBEY (*Increasingly bewildered*) What's that?

WILLIE I'll explain that too.

TOBEY All right. (*The sound of the streetcar has been heard, growing louder during the last few speeches. It comes to a halt in front of No. 31*) Somebody's getting off. Could it be my mother?
    (*He jumps off the stoop and goes part way up the hill*)

43

WILLIE Oh, no. She's not expected yet.

TOBEY (*Disappointed, peers through the gloom*) It's only a girl!
    (*He comes back to the steps*)

WILLIE (*Peering also*) Maybe it's Leah from Fitchburg. (LEAH, *carrying a cheap suitcase, walks into the shaft of light that comes from the tenement windows.* WILLIE *jumps to his feet.* LEAH *is an extremely attractive young girl. To* LEAH) Can I help you, miss?

LEAH I'm looking for a Mrs. Feinberg.

WILLIE Are you, by any chance, from Fitchburg?

LEAH (*Surprised*) Yes. How did you know?

WILLIE (*Jumps off stoop*) I'm Sherlock Holmes! Mrs. Feinberg lives right there on the left. She's expecting you. (*Gallantly*) You see! Your reputation has preceded you!

LEAH (*Shyly*) Thank you.

WILLIE I'm Willie Lavin.

LEAH I'm very glad to meet you.

WILLIE This is Tobey.

LEAH (*Smiles at him*) Hello, Tobey.

WILLIE   Here, let me have your suitcase.

LEAH   Oh, thank you!

WILLIE   From what I hear—congratulations are in order.

LEAH   (*Intensely embarrassed*)   Really? Why?

WILLIE   (*Not noticing*)   May I say that the gentleman from Atlanta is a very lucky man?
       (*Her agitation is now so pronounced that* WILLIE *does notice*)

LEAH   Oh, Mr. Lavin—I—I—

WILLIE   (*Concerned*)   Do you feel faint, Miss—?

LEAH   —Long. I just felt a bit dizzy—I don't know why . . .

WILLIE   Here—sit down a minute . . .

LEAH   (*Accepts*)   Thank you.
       (*She sits on the stoop*)

WILLIE   It's a long ride from Fitchburg. Were you, by any chance, carsick?

LEAH   Oh, no—it's just that—it's bewildering after Fitchburg to find myself in this big city all of a sudden—and—and—

WILLIE   As a bride? To a man you've never met. (LEAH *does not answer. She is miserable.* WILLIE *sees it*) I'm sorry if I—

45

TOBEY (*Cuts in*)   Worcester is built on seven hills, you know. Like Rome. Rome was built on seven hills.

LEAH (*Smiles at him*)   Was it?

TOBEY   The highest is Mount Wachusett. You can see it from almost any place. I've been to the top twice. Willie can we take her to the top of Mount Wachusett?

WILLIE   Sure, why not?

LEAH   I'd love to go.

WILLIE   Fine. We'll go.

LEAH   You are the son of Lavin and Lupkin, aren't you?

WILLIE (*With suave pomposity*)   That is an approximate statement. More accurately I am the son of Mr. Lavin, who is the senior partner of Lavin and Lupkin. Biologically speaking, I have no relationship whatever to Mr. Lupkin.

LEAH (*She laughs*)   You are very funny.

WILLIE (*After a moment*)   The gossip has it that the lucky gentleman is a very well-off citizen of Atlanta, Georgia.

LEAH (*Acutely embarrassed*)   I see everybody knows it. That only makes it worse!

WILLIE (*Comes right to the point*)   Have you got cold feet, Leah?

Susanne Pleshette and Eli Wallach, as LEAH and WILLIE

LEAH   Oh, Mr. Lavin . . .

WILLIE   Willie.

LEAH   Oh, Willie, I feel *so ungrateful!*

WILLIE   (*Cracks his knuckles*)   I can very well imagine a situation where at the very altar . . . (*Firmly*) Where, at the very altar, the bride will relinquish the groom. I will go so far as to say . . . that unless the impulse toward this person is *overwhelming* it is your *duty* to break off this engagement.

LEAH   But Ida has been so kind and for a stranger, you might say. She hardly knows me. She's taken *so* much trouble.

WILLIE   Ida, out of the goodness of her heart, has found husbands for the halt, the lame and the blind—she will have no problem whatever with you, Leah.

TOBEY   (*Proudly*)   Ida's my aunt.

LEAH   Is she?

TOBEY   Oh, yes. Isn't she, Willie?

WILLIE   Beyond the shadow of a doubt.

LEAH   (*Gets up. Impulsively she kisses* TOBEY. *To* WILLIE)   I can't tell you how much better you've made me feel. You've taken such a load off my mind. I only hope I have the courage to—to . . .

47

WILLIE (*Rises*) Tell you what I'll do. In a few minutes I'll look in on you at Ida's. If you haven't summoned the courage to tell her by that time, I'll do it for you.

LEAH I can't tell you how grateful I am!

WILLIE It is the highest function of human beings to help each other—especially in moments of crisis. I venture to say that the opportunity may some day come for *you* to help *me*.

LEAH Oh, I hope it does.
(NORBERT MANDEL *comes walking up the hill, swaggering and complacent. He carries a cane. He is around forty. He has a ginger-colored mustache—which he twirls elegantly, especially when he is meditating something—and ginger-colored, thinning hair*)

WILLIE *and* TOBEY Good evening, Mr. Mandel.
(MANDEL *nods condescendingly*)

MANDEL Good evening. Enjoying the moonlight?
(*He notices* LEAH)

WILLIE This is Miss Long just arrived from Fitchburg.

MANDEL Good evening, Miss Long.

LEAH Good evening.

MANDEL Are you the bride of the lucky gentleman from Atlanta?

48

LEAH (*Greatly embarrassed*)   Well, I don't know . . .

MANDEL   I am Norbert Mandel. I am the proprietor of this property. My own residence is just on the top of the hill, very noticeable by its stain-glass window.

LEAH   How nice.

MANDEL   I am a close personal friend of Mrs. Feinberg and had I known she had so charming a client Norbert Mandel would have expressed a personal interest.

LEAH (*In agony*)   Thank you.

MANDEL   I have just completed the purchase of a Winton Six. Consider it will be at your service any time should you care to see our fair countryside. Good night.
    (MANDEL *continues his stately progress up the hill*)

LEAH   Oh, dear. Everybody knows about it and now if it doesn't happen, what will Mrs. Feinberg say?

WILLIE   Don't worry about Ida. I will straighten it out with her.

LEAH   Well, I'd better be going up. Ida will be wondering. Which floor is it?

WILLIE   I'll show you.
    (WILLIE *leads* LEAH *up the steps to the main door, carrying her suitcase*)

LEAH   And you'll really come?

WILLIE   You may count on me.

LEAH   That's wonderful!

WILLIE   By that time you will have crossed the Rubicon. If not
—I'll cross it for you.
(WILLIE *holds the front door open as he hands her her
suitcase, and points the direction of* IDA'*s door*)

WILLIE (*Looking after* LEAH)   I venture the opinion that that
is a very estimable young lady. Well, Tobey! Up with you.
You've got to go to bed.

TOBEY (*As they disappear into the hallway*)   Willie, what's the
Rubicon?

WILLIE   Right through here—
(*The lights dim down on stoop and come up in* IDA'*s
room.* LEAH *has knocked on* IDA'*s door.* IDA, *crossing her
parlor, lets* LEAH *in. She greets her warmly*)

IDA   Come! Leah darling! I was beginning to get worried
there was an accident with the streetcar.

LEAH   Oh, no. Everything was fine. (*Looks around*) What a
beautiful tenement!

IDA   That's your room, and there's the piazza. (*Points*) There
from the piazza you can see the whole world.

LEAH (*Goes out on the piazza and looks down the street. As she comes back into the room—*)   I met your nephew.

IDA   Tobey?

LEAH   Yes.

IDA   So if you met Tobey you met Willie Lavin. If Tobey were Willie's own son he couldn't take more care. And how did you like Willie?

LEAH   He's a darling!

IDA (*As a brilliant idea strikes her*)   He's very educated from the chemistry. To meet Willie Lavin that's a good start. I want you should have a good time in Worcester. You want perhaps to lie down for a nap after your trip?

LEAH (*Has decided to take the plunge*)   Before I do anything— I want to talk to you about . . . about . . .

IDA   About the furrier from Atlanta.

LEAH (*Faces her, prepared to speak the truth*)   Yes. I do.
        (*She sits on the sofa*)

IDA (*Sits beside her*)   So we'll talk. But first, Leah darling, I owe you an apology.

LEAH   Why?

IDA   Because about that furrier from Atlanta I found out such things that I apologize I ever got you mixed up with such a no-good.

LEAH (*Feels greatly relieved*)   Really?

IDA (*Squaring off*)   It's a miracle I found out in time. It's like a special delivery from God.

LEAH   What did you find out?

IDA   In the first place I met somebody who knows him close and his face is with pimples. In the photograph you can't see because the photographer took them all out with an eraser. This is right away dishonest. In his leg he has a vein. And, over and above, he's not even a furrier. What he sells is from cats. So now the mayor of Atlanta is after him with a subpoena.

LEAH (*Happy to be absolved, playing along*)   Then how can I face him when he comes tomorrow?

IDA (*By this time she firmly believes everything she is saying; her eyes flash with righteous indignation*)   You think I would let a no-good low-life that steals cats set foot in this house? Today I sent him a telegram he should save himself the trouble.

LEAH (*Who could cry out for joy*)   To tell you the truth, I'm relieved.

IDA   Relieved is nothing. You are salvaged!

52

LEAH   I do want to get married. But somehow—I want . . .

IDA   You'll get!

LEAH *(Smiles at her)*   Let's hope.

IDA   Take my word.

LEAH   Ida—it just occurred to me . . . now that the furrier is *not* coming, there's no reason really for me to stay here.

IDA   Stay you will for the company. Here are people coming and going. In the afternoon we go to Easton's Drug Store— five o'clock it's full of prospects with milk shakes. Already you met Willie Lavin. I bet he right away melted.

LEAH *(Laughs, picks up suitcase)*   Well, all right, if you'll put up with me.

IDA *(Opens bedroom door for LEAH)*   In here is your room.

LEAH *(Surveying it from threshold)*   How pretty!

IDA   The flowers my daughter picked. Yellow I like in flowers, don't you? *(She closes the door after LEAH, and walks back into the parlor. She is full of thoughts, plans for LEAH. WILLIE comes in)* Willie, for you I have the most wonderful news.

WILLIE   What about?

IDA   Leah from Fitchburg is free.

WILLIE (*Teasing her*) What about the furrier from Atlanta?

IDA She don't like his picture. Already she sent a telegram to the furrier he should stay where he is!

WILLIE Well, I'm glad that's disposed of. (*A moment; he doesn't have to help out* LEAH *now*) I think I'll go home and do some work.

(*He starts toward door.* IDA, *in a panic that he will leave without seeing* LEAH, *grabs him by the arm*)

IDA Leah darling. Willie Lavin is here!

(LEAH *comes back*)

LEAH Oh, Mr. Lavin, how nice of you to remember . . .

IDA So why shouldn't he remember? A girl like you the problem is not to remember, the problem is to forget.

(IDA *goes out into the kitchen.* LEAH *and* WILLIE *find themselves embarrassed at being left alone together*)

WILLIE (*Awkwardly*) Well, Leah! Was the ordeal as formidable as you expected?

LEAH It wasn't an ordeal. Ida did it all. I can't tell you what a relief it is not to be a bride! (*An awkward pause, as she sits on the sofa*) You know, I've never slept away from home before in my whole life.

WILLIE (*Sitting beside her*) Really?

LEAH It's a strange experience. I'm so excited I don't see how I ever will fall asleep tonight.

WILLIE Under other circumstances I would take you to White City. That's what we call our Amusement Park on the Lake. There's dancing.

LEAH I'd love to go sometime.

WILLIE I'll be happy to take you. It's just that tonight I—I have to get up early for a very important exam—I'm a senior, you know, at Worcester Polytechnic Institute.

LEAH (*Rises.* WILLIE *gets up*) Of course. I understand perfectly. You've been more than kind to me already. I can't tell you how grateful I am.
(*At this moment we see* MYRA *on her balcony and* DAN *on the stoop below. She calls down to him*)

MYRA I hate your leaving so early, darling.

DAN Got to be at the office early—got to be on my toes from now on—for my honey!
(DAN *waves to* MYRA *and disappears up the hill.* MYRA *leans over her balcony for a moment*)

MYRA Willie—Willie—
(*On hearing* MYRA's *voice,* WILLIE *dashes across the room, out on the piazza, and looks up at* MYRA)

WILLIE Excuse me, Miss Long . . . Myra . . .

55

MYRA   Who're you with? Who're you talking to?

WILLIE   Ida's house guest. A Miss Long.

MYRA   Oh, Willie, I'm sad. I'm lonely.

WILLIE   Where's Dan?

MYRA   He got tired. He's gone home. Please come and talk to me.

WILLIE   Be right there! (*He has forgotten all about* LEAH—*remembers her only when he sees her as he runs back into the room from the piazza*) Oh, excuse me, Miss Long! (*Lamely*) It's an old friend of mine who lives upstairs . . .
> (*He runs out.* LEAH *looks after him a moment, then she goes out to the piazza and leans over the rail to peer out into the darkness to catch a glimpse of the siren. When* LEAH *comes back into the room, her expression is wistful. She feels very lonely suddenly. She calls out*)

LEAH   Ida! Ida!
> (IDA *bustles in*)

IDA   Where's Willie?

LEAH   A friend of his called him from upstairs. He went up to talk to her.

IDA   Myra?

LEAH   Yes. That's her name. Myra. I couldn't see in the dark. Is she attractive?

IDA (*With contempt*) She's thin and she giggles.

LEAH Well, I guess she's attractive enough to make Willie forget his important examination tomorrow morning.
(IDA *comes to* LEAH *full of sympathy and understanding,
and comforts her*)

IDA Leah, darling, about that hitzel-dritzel you don't have to
worry, Leah, because in two weeks she's getting married!

The Curtain Falls

ACT TWO

ACT TWO

Scene One

Two years later.
At rise, TOBEY *and* MR. SACHER *are in* IDA'S *parlor.*

FATHER   Well, Tobey, I have to be getting back to the grocery! (*Sighs*) Though why I don't know.

TOBEY   Is business bad?

FATHER   It's not flourishing! Well, there's one consolation, Tobey, in running an unsuccessful grocery. You can eat the inventory.

TOBEY   Ida is very kind to us—having us to meals and everything—but I miss Mother. I dream at night that she is alive—then I wake up.

FATHER   I know, Tobey. So do I.

TOBEY (*Under great strain*)   Father!

FATHER   Yes, Tobey.

TOBEY   There's something I've got to tell you!

FATHER   What is it, Tobey?

TOBEY   I've done a terrible thing—a crime—

FATHER   Can it be so serious?

TOBEY   I broke my glasses again last week.

FATHER   Did you? You didn't tell me.

TOBEY   I was ashamed to tell you. I've broken them so often. I
know things are not easy for you—and it's fifty cents a lens.

FATHER   How did you get the money to replace them?

TOBEY   That's what's so terrible. I stole it.

FATHER   From the till?

TOBEY   No. I wouldn't do that!

FATHER   How then?

TOBEY   The Sweet Caporal packs from your shelves.

FATHER   Oh—you sold the cigarettes?

TOBEY   No, Father. The pictures. You know they have those
pictures inside. Prize fighters like Bob Fitzsimmons and Jim
Corbett. Allie Seidenberg is collecting the prize fighters. He
needed Joe Choynski desperately. He offered me one dollar
for Joe Choynski.

FATHER   A dollar for Joe Choynski?

62

TOBEY So—I—

FATHER Yes, Tobey?

TOBEY I ripped open a dozen packs till I found Joe Choynski.

FATHER Prize fighters? Why is trained violence so idealized? Why don't they put pictures in the cigarette packs of the philosophers: Spinoza, Descartes, Maimonides?

TOBEY I guess they're not so well known, Father. I'm sorry, Father. I felt I had to tell you.

FATHER (*Absently*) Thou shalt not steal.

TOBEY I'll never do it again, Father.

FATHER It would have been better if you'd asked me for money, Tobey. Cheaper, too.
(*He starts to go.* WILLIE *comes in. He has just come from* MYRA'S *upstairs*)

WILLIE It's not to be believed what I hear.

FATHER What do you hear?

WILLIE The minute Dan died you all began to back Aaron's claim to marry Myra. And you justify it by invoking a dead law.

FATHER Why do you accuse me?

WILLIE I've just left Myra's mother. She says you approve of this monstrous engagement—(WILLIE *goes to* TOBEY, *and harangues* MR. SACHER *through* TOBEY) Imagine, Tobey, you live

63

in a community where they marry girls off by medieval rites. Now, in Worcester, Massachusetts in nineteen ten.

FATHER   Now, Willie—I hate to contradict a scientist because naturally scientists know everything, but you're wrong about this law. It's not medieval. It's Biblical.

WILLIE   Even remoter.

FATHER   You'll find it in the book of Ruth. I looked at it just this morning. (*He quotes*) "Moreover Ruth the Moabitess have I purchased to be my wife . . . that the name of the dead be not cut off from among his brethren, and from the gate of his place."

WILLIE   Exactly. Purchased. It was a real estate deal then. It's a real estate deal now.

FATHER   You simplify too much. There is a deeper reality behind it; a desire for immortality. Don't you see what threatens Mr. Eisner? That his name will be cut off from among his brethren and from the gate of his place.

WILLIE   It is brutal of Mr. Eisner to gratify his desire for immortality at Myra's expense. I'm studying law now and I've gone into this thing. Actually this law gives Myra the right to accept Aaron or refuse him. *She* has the right.

FATHER   That is so. But why are you so impassioned about this, Willie? Let Myra do what she wants.

WILLIE   Two years ago you stopped me from telling Myra the truth about Dan. With what result? Suffering and early widowhood for Myra.

FATHER   I ask you now what I asked you then—what is the motive behind your crusade?

WILLIE   All right. It's selfish. I love Myra. I intend to marry Myra. Had I behaved selfishly two years ago I'd have saved Myra from a horror that has left its mark. Good would have come from an impure motive. Your rigid code has resulted in disaster.

FATHER   (*With humor*)   Myra is adaptable. She'll get over it.

WILLIE   I'll see that she does!

FATHER   Willie—Willie—you've thrown over chemistry—now you're studying law—you change your profession over night. But about Myra you're steadfast. I wish it were the other way round. (*A moment*) Well, I've got to get back to the grocery. Tobey, I am disturbed by what you told me. I thought I was selling cigarettes. I didn't know I was selling prize fighters.
   (*He goes out*)

TOBEY   (*To* WILLIE)   Father's so impractical. He doesn't know his own stock.

WILLIE   Tobey. I'm all worked up. Let's go for a walk.

TOBEY   Love to!
   (IDA *comes in from the kitchen*)

WILLIE   (*With affectionate reproach*)   You too, Ida. You too.

IDA   I too what?

WILLIE Myra's mother tells me you're on her side. (*Goes to her, pinches her cheek*) You too invoke the levirate law against me.

IDA From laws I know nothing. I go by what is good for you, Willie, and to get Myra safely settled with Aaron would be a load off. Aaron I hope is healthy enough to stay for a while.

WILLIE (*Laughs to* TOBEY) No getting around Ida, Tobey. She pursues an objective with the tenacity of a—with the tenacity of a—(*Hung up*) Of a what, Tobey?

TOBEY With tenacity.

WILLIE You see!
(*They go out through the kitchen as* MANDEL, *the land-lord, knocks loudly and comes in. He is in smart riding costume: boots, whipcord breeches. He wears a carna-tion in the lapel of his tweed jacket, and carries a riding crop which he swishes occasionally, with nonchalance.* IDA *is in a fluster at seeing* MANDEL)

IDA Mandel! What a happy surprise!

MANDEL Mrs. Feinberg.
(IDA *stares in admiration at* MANDEL, *taking in every de-tail of his bizarre costume*)

IDA Tell me, Mandel, in this suit are you coming or going?

MANDEL Going.

IDA It is a pleasure to look on you, Mandel. You smell from solid leather!

66

MANDEL (*Formally*) Thank you for the compliment, Mrs. Feinberg.

IDA So tell me, with this suit where are you going?

MANDEL Sundays is usual with me horseback. Sundays I canter. I am a habitue.

IDA (*Stares at him, rapt*) A peace on you, Mandel!

MANDEL Thank you for the thought, but peace I don't want. Peace I'll have in my grave. Norbert Mandel wants action! (*He swishes his riding crop, by way of action*)

IDA (*Drinking him in with adoration*) A long life to you, Mandel!

MANDEL (*With restraint*) Thank you, Mrs. Feinberg. Does Miss Long happen to be home?

IDA No. Leah went out.

MANDEL That's too bad because now I have an appointment with my groom.

IDA Before the groom let me give you a piece of fish.

MANDEL Thank you, Mrs. Feinberg, but before a canter I never eat.

IDA But, Mandel! Why are you so formal? In the letter you wrote me from Revere Beach you call me Ida dear.

MANDEL (*Swishing idly*) In all the world—yes, I think I can say it Mrs. Feinberg—in all the world there is no woman I hold in the high regards I hold you.

IDA So what interrupts?

MANDEL (*Enjoys a Byronic melancholy—rotates his riding crop slowly*) My experience of life has been so sad, dear friend. My wife—may-she-rest-in-peace—the good Lord took away. So I have decided from henceforth to concentrate on riding, hunting and real estate developments.

IDA You are a young man yet—in the prime.

MANDEL Norbert Mandel is old through suffering.

IDA Mandel—listen to me—

MANDEL (*Very cagey*) Yes, dear one?

IDA I have decided I would like, for a change, to be a private woman!

MANDEL (*Affected incredulity*) Give up matchmaking! You wouldn't. It's in your blood.

IDA You should get married, Mandel—even if it's not me!

MANDEL Is this your true opinion?

IDA Whose true opinion isn't it?

MANDEL Then I must tell you of a strange development that has developed lately in my psychology.

IDA What development?

MANDEL I am attracted, Mrs. Feinberg.

IDA (*Dashed but game*) By whom are you attracted?

MANDEL (*Takes the plunge*) Your lodger—Miss Long.

IDA (*Flabbergasted*) Leah!

MANDEL Yes.

IDA But Leah is a young girl—a child!

MANDEL But didn't you just admit that I am in the prime?

IDA (*With some heat*) Even for the prime Leah is too young. Leah is in the beginning. Besides—for Leah I am already arranging.

MANDEL (*Hard*) The fact is, Mrs. Feinberg . . .

IDA So what is the fact?

MANDEL (*Tensely—Byron is cast away; Don Juan replaces him*) The fact is that in Norbert Mandel your lodger arouses the flame.

IDA At our age let me tell you from the shoulder, Mandel, marriage is no flame.

MANDEL (*Swishes, flamelike*) For less Norbert Mandel will not settle!

69

IDA (*Fighting a losing action*)   At our age a good marriage is to have steam heat in winter and an icebox in the summer.
(LEAH *comes in; she is surprised to see* MANDEL)

LEAH   Oh, Mr. Mandel. How are you?

MANDEL   Happy to see you, Miss Long.

LEAH (*To* IDA)   I just bumped into Willie Lavin and Tobey. Willie asked me to White City tonight.

IDA (*Rises. Gives* MANDEL *a meaningful look*)   You see, Mandel! A fine canter to you, Mandel.

MANDEL   Thank you, Mrs. Feinberg. (IDA *goes out into the kitchen. For a few moments there is an awkward silence between* LEAH *and* MANDEL. *Finally—*) Do you ride horseback, Miss Long?

LEAH (*Smiles*)   I'm afraid that's not for the likes of me, Mr. Mandel. I'm a working girl.

MANDEL   I have kept you under my eye for some time, Miss Long.

LEAH (*Surprised*)   Have you?

MANDEL   You are a bright girl. Give you the opportunity you could shine in a bigger world than Providence Street.

LEAH   But I'm not ambitious to. I like Providence Street. Providence Street has been very good to me! (*A moment*) And now—if you'll excuse me, I'm afraid I'll have to . . .
(*She starts toward the door of her room*)

70

MANDEL (*Takes her arm as she starts to go*) May I ask you something, Miss Long—something personal?

LEAH Certainly.

MANDEL May I ask how it happens—a lovely person like you— how it happens you are *not* married?

LEAH (*Smiles at him*) That is very simple to answer, Mr. Mandel. No one has ever asked me.

MANDEL (*Ravished by her smile, touched by her candor*) You are an honest soul, Miss Long—a very unusual soul.

LEAH (*Embarrassed*) Well—thank you.
(*She starts to go again, but he holds her*)

MANDEL (*Very tense*) No one, you say, has ever asked you?

LEAH That's right.

MANDEL I ASK YOU, MISS LONG!

LEAH (*Startled*) Surely, Mr. Mandel—you're not serious . . .

MANDEL (*Still holding her arm*) Norbert Mandel was never so serious in his life! I am in the prime of life, Miss Long . . .

LEAH Congratulations!

MANDEL I am able to satisfy your heart's desire—every which way. Give me yes and in a week you are living like a queen. You will find out that Norbert Mandel is a man of action. He don't let the grass grow.

LEAH (*Rises*)   It is only fair to tell you—I am in love.

MANDEL   Willie Lavin? (*Cruel, inexorable, triumphant*) Now that Myra is a widow you will get no place with Willie Lavin!

LEAH (*Angry at him for saying this hard truth, and taking her own revenge*)   In any case, I could never marry you.

MANDEL   And why not? Do you intend, perhaps, to remain an old maid?

LEAH   Rather than marry you—yes!
(*On the verge of tears she runs into her room.* MR. MANDEL *is dumfounded, furious. He swishes his riding crop savagely. With his free hand he twirls his mustache in anger*)

MANDEL (*Suddenly calling out in a voice of thunder*)   MRS. FEINBERG!
(IDA *comes in*)

IDA   What's the matter? The house caught fire?

MANDEL   I AM ON FIRE, MRS. FEINBERG!

IDA   From the flame?

MANDEL   Yes, the FLAME. I am in the prime and in the prime the flame burns hotter than in the beginning!

IDA   So what do you want I should do?

MANDEL   Arrange for me with Leah Long, and Norbert Mandel will never forget you!

72

IDA   It's a funny way, Mandel, to preserve me in your mind!

MANDEL   For your benefit, Mrs. Feinberg, I can tell you in confidence—recently I took out a big policy with the Prudential Insurance Company.

IDA   You're sick, Mandel?

MANDEL   Norbert Mandel was never in better health in his life. But get me yes from Miss Long and overnight she becomes the beneficiary. On my policies with the Prudential Insurance Company is featured a big rock. Norbert Mandel is like that rock. Stable. Gilt-edged. Pass that to Miss Long; she should know on which side is the butter.

IDA   I'll pass.

MANDEL   Good day, Mrs. Feinberg!
   (*He goes*)

LEAH (*After he goes, from her room*)   Has he gone?

IDA   Gone he has. And, Leah, you should know if the worst, God forbid, comes to the worst, you have in reserve a BIG ROCK!
   (*The lights dim out and come up on the stoop. We see* MYRA *on the piazza, looking anxiously up and down the street. We see* MANDEL's *majestic exit. He encounters* WILLIE *and* TOBEY *on the stoop*)

WILLIE   Hello, Mr. Mandel.

MANDEL   Hello, hello.
   (*He goes quickly up the hill*)

73

MYRA Willie! I've been waiting for you!

WILLIE I'll be right up.

MYRA No. I'll come down. Mother's nagging the life out of me. I'll be there in a moment.

TOBEY Willie?

WILLIE Yes.

TOBEY Before you go on this big fight, your object is to marry Myra. Right?

WILLIE (*Humoring him*) That is the dazzling objective—yes.

TOBEY Don't you think then, that the *first* thing you should do is to find out how Myra feels? Oughtn't that to be the first step?

WILLIE (*With the same tone of raillery*) My impetuosity is so great that I'm taking the second step first.

TOBEY (*Knows he is being chaffed*) Seriously, Willie!

WILLIE Seriously—Myra or no Myra—I've got to upset the CONCEPT—the concept of the dead hand. (*Thunder and lightning, the promise of a storm*) Applause from Heaven! (*He sits on the bench*)

TOBEY (*Sitting beside him*) I love before a storm. Willie, I want to tell you something: when I play the piano—Schubert and Chopin—

74

WILLIE Well?

TOBEY I think of Leah. The music's like Leah.

WILLIE I see what you mean, Tobey. Leah's a wonderful girl.
Loyal, self-reliant—

TOBEY Isn't that a lot?

WILLIE There's no mystery in Leah—in Myra there's mystery.

TOBEY What's mysterious about Myra?

WILLIE That's part of the chemistry of sex. Unexplainable.

TOBEY Spontaneous combustion?

WILLIE That's right.

TOBEY (*Shyly*) If I were older, Willie—

WILLIE Yes, Tobey?

TOBEY Well, I'd get more combustion out of Leah. I think
about her at night.

WILLIE Do you? It used to be the Dark Angel and holding on
to the bedposts.

TOBEY I've forgotten about them. It's Leah now.

WILLIE That's progress.

TOBEY It's troublesome too. (*A moment*) I just don't understand, Willie, why you don't love Leah.

WILLIE Neither do I, Tobey!

TOBEY If things don't turn out—between you and Myra—will you turn to Leah?

WILLIE Things *must* turn out for me and Myra.

TOBEY One reason I love Leah is because she thinks you're wonderful. And when I talk to Myra about you—

WILLIE Yes?

TOBEY We always end up talking about Myra.
      (MYRA *appears on the stoop*)

MYRA Hello, Tobey.

WILLIE Well, go on up and practice your piece. (TOBEY *reluctantly goes*) Where do you want to go?

MYRA Anywhere . . . (*It begins to rain hard. Thunder and lightning. She shrinks against him for protection*) Oh, Willie. I just can't stand the thunder. It frightens me so!

WILLIE (*Holds her to him, adoring it*) It isn't the thunder that's dangerous—it's the lightning that's dangerous. There— you see—it's over. It's just a summer shower . . .
      (*There is another great thunderclap. She buries her face against the lapel of his coat, stopping her ears with her hands*)

MYRA Oh, Willie—I'm so scared!

76

WILLIE (*Holding her*)   You were afraid of thunder. Since you were a little girl.
(*A sudden lightning flash illuminates the stoop*)

MYRA (*Removes her hands from her ears*)   Is it over?

WILLIE   Over. Now it's just the rain. Remember that awful thunderstorm—when we were out canoeing—a few years ago. Remember how scared you were! And you lived through it, didn't you?

MYRA   I remember *every* thunderstorm. Ever since I was a kid —they drove me crazy with fear.

WILLIE   I paddled to shore—we turned the canoe over—and lay under it—remember? Remember the noise the rain made on the canoe bottom—like bullets?

MYRA   I remember how wonderful it was when it went away.

WILLIE   I remember how wonderful it was—lying close to you.

MYRA (*A little calmer now; there is the sound of steady rain*) I know it's silly. Why is it? Why am I so scared?

WILLIE (*Cracks his knuckles*)   I venture to say that if you analyzed it to its source you'd find some deep psychic . . .

MYRA (*Interrupts him*)   Willie, why do you crack your knuckles like that? You're always doing it. Why?

WILLIE (*Turning it off adroitly*)   Perhaps for the same reason you're afraid of thunder.
(*They both laugh a little*)

77

MYRA (*Sitting on the bench*) Ever since Dan died—everything scares me even more. And now this with Aaron—and he's coming here any minute.

WILLIE (*Sitting beside her*) Why should you throw yourself away on somebody you don't love like Aaron?

MYRA When it comes to that, I'd rather marry you than marry Aaron.

WILLIE That's cold comfort!

MYRA (*A moment*) Sometimes I think of running away.

WILLIE Where would you go?

MYRA New York. I love New York. When I was there with Dan I met the manager of the Hotel Astor. Imagine—the manager!

WILLIE Did he fall in love with you too?

MYRA Oh, no. He's fat and old and has hundreds of children. But Dan fell ill—and this manager was so very kind. He said: if you want a job in New York, let me know.
(*We hear* TOBEY *playing Chopin*)

WILLIE But, Myra, I've waited for you.

MYRA I know. I used to think—during that dreadful time— Willie loves me—Willie's waiting for me.

WILLIE Did you, darling? Did you know?

MYRA Of course I knew, and it consoled me. I thought—he's waiting—and I'm waiting.

WILLIE For me? Were you waiting for me?

MYRA I'm always waiting for a promise. That no one made me but which I've always felt. It's a kind of a feeling that there is—there must be—love—which will make life—which will somehow make life . . .

WILLIE (*Suddenly miserable*) I think I know what you mean.

MYRA But *with* the promise I'm afraid of the future too—as if it were thunder.

WILLIE I'll protect you from the thunder, Myra.

MYRA Come closer to me. Talk to me, Willie. Tell me your innermost thoughts. (*He obeys her. He is tongue-tied, in an ecstasy of love*) Say something to me—something soothing like the rain.

WILLIE I love you. I've never loved anyone else. I never will love anyone else.

MYRA How can you tell that?

WILLIE I know it.

MYRA What about Leah?

WILLIE Leah's not you! No one in the whole world is you.

MYRA Are you going to marry Leah?

79

WILLIE   How can I when it's you I love?

MYRA   Willie—Willie darling—

WILLIE   (*Downcast, knows what's coming*)   Yes, Myra?

MYRA   I love you. But shall I tell you something? Don't wait for me. Love me. Don't forget me ever. But don't wait for me.

WILLIE   No matter what you say, I'll wait for you. Always.

MYRA   I hate this mourning dress. Don't look at it. I feel that I'm pretending more than I feel when I wear mourning for Dan. I hate mourning like I hate the dark. I love light. I love bright colors. Oh, I'd love to be gay for you, Willie.

WILLIE   Be gay. Go up and change your dress.

MYRA   Oh, I'd be afraid to.

WILLIE   Don't be. Go up and change.

MYRA   I will. Why shouldn't I? I will.
(*She goes in.* AARON *enters from the right, holding an umbrella. He is sullen and attempts to brush by* WILLIE *without speaking to him.* WILLIE *seizes his arm, holds him*)

WILLIE   I want to talk to you, Aaron—seriously.

AARON   I don't want to talk to you. I dislike you.

WILLIE   I know that and I understand it. But I think for both our sakes we should declare an armistice and have a council of war.

AARON   What are you driving at?

WILLIE   Our tactics with Myra. I think they are wrong.

AARON   I have no tactics. My case is clear.

WILLIE   It may be clear but it has one defect. Myra doesn't consider you have a case at all. Don't you see, Aaron, we've both made a serious mistake. We have to change our whole plan of attack.

AARON   Why do you say we? I'm marrying Myra. You're not.

WILLIE   She'll marry neither of us if we don't change our tactics. You are basing your whole claim on this old law. I am basing mine on demolishing the law. We are both misguided, Aaron, and do you know why? Because Myra is lawless. She is ruled by instinct, not by laws. We have to drop our present campaign—regroup our forces—we—

AARON   Stop saying we! Stop saying our! This isn't a joint enterprise!

WILLIE   It is a joint enterprise until one of us eliminates the other.
        (MYRA *comes back in a yellow dress.* AARON *is horrified*)

MYRA   Oh, Aaron.

AARON   (*In a terrible voice*)   What are you doing in that dress?

MYRA   Why I just—Willie said I could stop mourning for an hour—

AARON My brother is hardly in his grave and you—you put on this dress to tempt Willie. You're a harlot!

WILLIE Tactics, Aaron—tactics!

AARON You leave Myra alone.

WILLIE I will when she asks me.

AARON I'm Dan's younger brother. I have the right. She's mine by law. Get out!

MYRA I never loved you, Aaron. And now I don't even like you any more. I don't care about the law.

AARON Put on your mourning dress. (*To* WILLIE) And you get out before I . . .
  (*There is a tremendous thunderclap. In terror,* MYRA *clings to* WILLIE)

MYRA Willie—don't leave me—don't leave me with him—

WILLIE Don't worry, darling. I won't leave you.

AARON (*His voice drops, menacing and quiet*) You'll pay for this—both of you. And I'm going up now to tell your mother!
  (*He goes into the house*)

MYRA (*Whispers to* WILLIE) Willie—I'm scared—

WILLIE (*Masterfully*) Don't worry . . . He's like the thunder, darling—noisy but not dangerous.

MYRA You are the only one who loves me— Don't leave me— please, darling, don't leave me.

82

WILLIE (*Quietly, happy, holding her in his arms, kissing her hair*) Never, Myra. Never, my love. I'll never leave you. (*As he caresses her hair, the sound of the rain fades and we hear the town clock strike six times*)

The Lights Dim Out

Scene Two

MR. SACHER'S ROOM, *late afternoon the next day. The parlor reveals a Rembrandtesque scene of* FATHER *and his fellow scholars at their annual session, celebrating the finishing of the reading of one of the books of the Talmud: the great, calf-bound volumes are propped up before each of the students, who are all men of* FATHER'S *age, or older: in their ordinary lives grocers, peddlers, petty artisans, tailors, but now, transmuted in their absorption, figures from a medieval print, with their skull caps, sober garments and absolute absorption, poring over the parchment-like pages. A cadenced warm hum comes from them: intermittent little flares of subdued argument in crises of interpretation; silence, then the hum again—it is a sound, not articulate speech. A Menorah, with lighted candles, furnishes the only—flickering—illumination.*

TOBEY *is sitting on the stoop, his head buried in a book.*

We hear WILLIE'S *whistle, his habitual signal to* TOBEY, *as he comes down the hill—the first notes of Beethoven's* Fifth Symphony.

WILLIE   Hello, Tobey. What are you up to?

TOBEY   Well, I thought of going to the lake with Allie and the boys as soon as my father gets through up there.

WILLIE   Oh, the annual session.

84

TOBEY Does it take them a whole year to go through one of those Talmud books, Willie?

WILLIE Well, they can only devote part time to it.

TOBEY What's in them anyway?

WILLIE (*Sitting beside him*) The Talmud? A code of law and behavior—interpretation. Some of it's very funny.

TOBEY Really? I never see my father or his friends laugh.

WILLIE Well, it's a serious business for them. For instance, there is a speculation: Why did God make Eve out of Adam's rib? Well, the Talmud suggests if he'd made her out of his hand she'd be grasping; if he'd made her out of his tongue she'd be a gossip; if he used his eyes she'd be overcurious. In addition, God wanted Eve to be modest. So he used the rib because it was invisible. So, he stuck to this neutral material, the rib, with the result that she is now grasping, gossipy, incessantly curious and of disturbing visibility.

TOBEY (*Laughing*) I wish those books were in English. I'd love to read them.

WILLIE You don't have time—not till you've finished that piece you're working on—*Opus One*.

TOBEY *Opus One*. I'll never finish it. I knew I'd never be a great pianist, Willie. Now I guess I'll never be a composer either.

WILLIE Stick to it. It'll come.

TOBEY   Are you free tonight?

WILLIE   No. I've got a date with Myra.

TOBEY   Everybody says Myra's given up Aaron for you.

WILLIE   So far, she's only given up Aaron.

TOBEY   Will she take you then?

WILLIE   That remains to be seen. You know Myra has an extraordinary faculty.

TOBEY   What's that?

WILLIE   She has the faculty of accepting you and rejecting you simultaneously.

(*Meanwhile, in the parlor there is a small final crisis of interpretation; the hum stops suddenly. Everyone's attention focuses on* FATHER; *obviously they look to him as the most learned, to bring them out of their dilemma. Complete silence.* FATHER *leans forward in concentration, his finger on the disputed passage. He repeats, reading the elusive sentence—first with one emphasis, then again with another, an entirely different emphasis. There is a sudden illumination among them; the difference in emphasis has dispelled the ambiguity, the meaning is now clear, irrefutable, to all of them. A great sigh of relief rises from the embattled table and then a kind of muted acclamation to* FATHER. *Laughter. Jubilation. They shut their books; they are like schoolboys released from an onerous task. Several of the men shake hands with* FATHER, *congratulating him.* MR. SACHER *goes out to the stoop in the gloaming*)

FATHER   Tobey—we're finished—come up—the tea and cakes —Tobey.

IDA   (*Comes out on the piazza. She sees* WILLIE *and* TOBEY *and* MR. SACHER) You heard the news? Your hitzel-dritzel, Myra.

WILLIE   (*Apprehensive*)   What happened?

IDA   She flew away the coop!

WILLIE   What do you mean?

IDA   She ran away. A note she left that she'll write a note. So why didn't she write it now? For you too she left a note.

WILLIE   Where is it?
            (WILLIE *starts up toward her*)

IDA   For the note you don't have to run because I read it!

WILLIE   You had no right to do that!

IDA   You, too, she tells when she gets settled she'll send you a note. What I have with Myra's mother I can't tell you. Dead Myra isn't I tell her. Better she should be dead she says.

WILLIE   I knew this would happen!

IDA   (*Matter-of-factly*)   So if you knew, why didn't you stop?

WILLIE   You've driven her out, all of you. The loveliest thing in this God-obsessed community—you've driven her out!

FATHER   No one forced Myra to go . . .

87

WILLIE (*In despair—really to himself*) All the bickering. All the wrangling. That fanatical father of Aaron's—Aaron himself.

FATHER (*Gently*) You are not fanatical, Willie. Could you keep her?

WILLIE I'll go to New York. She asked me never to leave her.

FATHER So then she promptly left you.

WILLIE (*As he goes up the hill*) I knew this would happen. I knew this would happen.

TOBEY (*Starting after him, stops*) Willie! Do you want me to come with you? Willie!

FATHER He needs solitude, Tobey. It's no reflection on you. He's had a terrible blow.

IDA No. It's a good blow. This blow will stop him from chasing that wild goose. Because don't you see, Tobey, for him Myra is no good. Now, I can arrange for him nice with Leah. (*She goes back into her house*)

TOBEY Father.

FATHER Yes, Tobey.

TOBEY Did you love Mother the way Willie loves Myra?

FATHER You don't love like that when you're older.

TOBEY But you did love Mother?

88

FATHER   Yes. I loved her very much.

TOBEY   Still you quarreled. I used to hear you quarreling. Mother never said anything. But your voice would go up— up—

FATHER   (*This makes him suffer*)   I am a sinful man, Tobey.

TOBEY   You pray all the time. You think about God all the time. That's why I could never understand about those quarrels.

FATHER   I suffer now over those quarrels. (*He stops, tries to explain*) Look, Tobey, your mother lived in a silent world. She had been in this country as long as I, and yet she never learned the language. I was a student when I married her— had never left our village. And then I went away to study more—in France and Germany—and when I came back—

TOBEY   Yes?

FATHER   Your mother was still a village girl. And I was arrogant and impatient! I wish that I could have— But it's too late now.

TOBEY   Father, do you think Willie will get over this?

FATHER   That's a question I can't answer, Tobey. When I see the troubles of the young, it's a positive relief to be old.

TOBEY   Father—is it possible, Father, to be in love without being unhappy?

FATHER It's possible, but highly unlikely.
(*He motions to* TOBEY *to come with him. They go into
the house*)

The Lights Dim Out

SCENE THREE

At IDA's, *a month later. There is a dress form with an attractive summer dress on it.* REN, *discontented, full of* Weltschmerz, *is on the piazza, surveying the passing scene. From the* SACHERS' *flat, we hear* TOBEY *struggling with a composition of his own:* Opus One. *We hear* ALLIE SEIDENBERG *whistling for* REN. REN *turns her back on him disdainfully, and comes into the room.*

IDA (*From the kitchen*)   Who is whistling?

REN (*With contempt*)   Allie Seidenberg is whistling.

IDA   So why don't you ask him to come up?

REN   Because he *disgusts* me, that's why!

IDA   Allie's father is a very fine man.

REN   His son isn't. He has a dirty mind.
     (IDA *enters from the kitchen, dressed to the nines in the style of Providence Street, 1910*)

IDA (*Shocked*)   Things like that you shouldn't say!

REN (*Very haughty*)   In school the other day he asked me what I was reading. I said, "The Lay of the Last Minstrel," and he made an offensive remark. I didn't even know what he meant!

IDA (*Mildly*)   So how do you know it wasn't nice?

91

REN (*Very lofty, very elegant*) By the tone!

IDA (*Putting on a large hat, an odd confection which blooms with cherries and other fruit*) You like my hat, Ren?

REN It's beautiful!
      (*They listen for a moment to a crescendo in* TOBEY's *composition*)

IDA That's Tobey practicing. You hear, Ren?

REN Oh, Ma, when are we moving to New York? I'm just stifled here.

IDA When your grandfather's second wife dies—may she live to be a hundred and twenty—but she won't—she has a lung —then I'll . . . (WILLIE *comes in. He employs his usual tone of jocular levity with* IDA *but he is under a cloud*) Oh, Willie, life!

WILLIE Why, Ida, you're dressed up like Queen Victoria. Where are you going?

IDA Tonight I have with the Ladies Burial Improvement Society. It's too late I tell them to improve but they like anyway to gossip. So where are you going?

WILLIE I have a date with Leah. We're going to White City.

IDA For a month already since Myra left you have dates with Leah, but where is the result? (*The sound of shrill whistle from the street.* REN *runs out to piazza.* IDA *explains to* WILLIE) Day and night they whistle for Ren.

WILLIE   Love call!
(REN *comes back and makes for the door*)

IDA   Who is it?

REN   Allie!
(IDA *is a bit surprised at* REN's *quick conversion.* WILLIE *listens to* TOBEY *playing upstairs*)

WILLIE (*Impressed*)   Say! Tobey's made progress.

IDA (*Points to the dress form*)   Look that dress Leah designed. Filene's in Boston want Leah should be a buyer.

WILLIE (*Abstracted*)   I shouldn't wonder. Leah is clever.

IDA   Moreandover—from Field Marshall in Chicago you heard? A store he has in Chicago they say bigger than Filene's. To him Leah sent a design. Right away she got a letter for an interview. From a good family he is that Field Marshall—so latch on quick to Leah before he sees her.

WILLIE (*Smiles at her*)   I adore Leah and it seems selfish somehow to interfere with such a brilliant match!

IDA   Yesterday Norbert Mandel came to see me.

WILLIE   Congratulations!

IDA   Don't scramble me up in my meaning. About Leah he came to see me. An expression from Florida he told me— Leah should fish or cut the bait. And to you too I tell the same thing, Willie—you shouldn't cut fish with Leah either.

WILLIE   Ida, darling, you're scrambling me up a bit—with your meaning.

IDA   What I mean you know.

WILLIE   I guess I do.

IDA   Did you hear, Willie—so crazy he is for Leah, Norbert Mandel, that last Sunday he fell off his horse!

WILLIE   I hope he recovered.

IDA   From the horse he recovered but from Leah he didn't recover!

WILLIE   (*Enjoys teasing her*)   Oh, now, Ida, you know perfectly well that Leah is far too nice a girl to take the august Mr. Mandel away from you. It wouldn't be ethical.

IDA   In this department I have news. For Leah too. Something important: TO NORBERT MANDEL I HAVE GROWN COOL! So now for Leah with Norbert is ethical.

WILLIE   But Ida! You astonish me. How can you fall in and out of love like that? You're volatile. You're capricious.

IDA   Don't bamble me with those high-tone words. This I tell you, Willie. Educated you are. Bright you're not!

WILLIE   Never was truer word spoken.

IDA   From that Myra you're still looning? On me her mother cries all the time. In the hotel in New York where she spent her honeymoon half-undressed she's selling cigarettes. In the

94

same hotel where she spent her honeymoon! Another hotel she couldn't find! About you, Willie, everybody on the hill is asking questions.

WILLIE (*Smiles*)   So am I!

IDA   Everybody is asking: he's good with the chemistry. Why does he all of a sudden switch to study for a lawyer?

WILLIE   Because I want to know for a lawyer.

IDA   Willie, I have loved you all your life—what is with you?

WILLIE   The surface is smooth. The interior's a bit untidy.

IDA   So everything tell to Leah. She'll fix.

WILLIE   I wonder.

IDA   If you won't tell Leah, at least tell me—in plain language.

WILLIE   The fact is, dear Ida, I am afflicted by a syndrome of perplexities. A syndrome, dear Ida—

IDA   Syndrome—pindrome, you've got to live!

WILLIE   That, darling, is the heart of my problem!
(LEAH *comes in from her room.* LEAH *and* WILLIE *greet each other warmly but with constraint*)

LEAH   Oh, hello, Willie.

WILLIE   Hello, Leah.

95

IDA (*Pointedly*)   Leah, Mandel was here. He plasters me where are you?

LEAH (*Smiles at her*)   I'm right here.

WILLIE   Have you heard, Leah? Ida has grown cool to Norbert Mandel!

IDA   Me with Mandel is a romantic dream.

WILLIE   What's wrong with a romantic dream?

IDA   It's no good in the daytime! And I tell you this Willie . . . You should stop cutting fish. And I tell both of you, it's a sin to live alone.
(*She goes out.* LEAH *and* WILLIE *look at each other, smiling*)

WILLIE   To be anchored to the bread and wine of life like Ida —to the near horizons—how enviable! Have you noticed? With Ida everything is factual—serious—a Heaven and Earth bounded by marriage.

LEAH (*Lightly*)   Well, what *are* Heaven and Earth bounded by? (*She is conscious that this may sound like a lead, changes the subject quickly*) Have you heard from Myra?

WILLIE   Once.

LEAH   In a whole month?

WILLIE   Well, she's very excited about being in New York. She's angling for a stage job. All the managers come to the Astor where she works.

96

LEAH Myra is so—seductive. Something wonderful's bound to happen to Myra.

WILLIE I hope so. (*Probing into his own mind, determined to be truthful*) I hope so—and I don't hope so.

LEAH What do you mean?

WILLIE I love Myra. And yet, way down deep in my heart, I want her *not* to succeed—in whatever she's after—so that *I'll* have a chance. Egotism. Selfish egotism.

LEAH (*After a moment*) Willie?

WILLIE Yes, Leah?

LEAH I am going to ask you something dreadful.

WILLIE You may ask me anything you like.

LEAH Did you have an affair with Myra?

WILLIE No. She wouldn't. She says if she'd sleep with me— she'd marry me. She's got something special about that. It was dreadful that way—I mean her experience with Dan—on their honeymoon . . . I gather it was something . . . she wants to forget about.

LEAH Now I'll tell *you* something awful . . . I'm relieved to hear you didn't have an affair with Myra. I was sure you did. I was jealous over that, terribly jealous. How's that for selfish egotism?

WILLIE You are a very fine person, Leah, I mean—to be so frank with me—to tell me about it . . .

LEAH Well—so did you! So *you* are a very nice person also! (WILLIE *looks at her, troubled.* LEAH *has lost self-control, she pushes on, savage*) That's what you are and that's what I am—what is Myra?
(*She is obeying compulsively a masochistic impulse*)

WILLIE (*Disconcerted*) What is Myra? Gosh, Leah, I don't know. It's like asking to describe a scent—an aroma. It's a kind of magic—a kind of . . .

LEAH (*Inexorable*) Well, what?

WILLIE She will say to you—she's so eager—she's so eager for sympathy, for understanding—she says—she always says . . .

LEAH Well?

WILLIE She'll say, "Shall I tell you something, Willie?" She's always saying that. It draws you into a kind of conspiracy with her, a cozy isolation, a secret shared only with her—from all the world . . .

LEAH Don't you imagine she says it to everybody?

WILLIE Of course. But that doesn't matter. But when she says it to you, then you're alone in the world with her. (*He is abashed at having said so much. Rises*) I don't know what it is, Leah—but you make me talk a lot of nonsense! Let's drop all this. Let's go to White City!

LEAH I don't think I feel like going any more.

98

WILLIE Oh, come on now, Leah—you can't go back on me like that—we have a date.
(*There is a moment of awkward silence between them. From upstairs we hear* TOBEY *practicing* Opus One)

LEAH It was very sweet of you, Willie, to give Tobey that piano.

WILLIE That's his own piece. I have an intuition about Tobey —that one day he'll do something. Tobey's creative. I'll study —he'll know. (*A pause*) It's only fair to tell you, Leah, I'm going to New York, for good.
(*The music fades out*)

LEAH When?

WILLIE Tomorrow. I have a feeling that Myra will one day come to a place where she'll need me—when that moment comes I must be there.

LEAH There'll be other men in Myra's life. You know that. I know that. You'll wait—you'll wait—for the parade to pass.

WILLIE Myra's vulnerable.

LEAH She does what she likes. She takes what she likes. What's vulnerable about Myra? (*She gets up and faces him. Passionately—she is not in control of herself*) Shall I tell you something, Willie? I'm glad you're going to New York. We've seen a lot of each other since Myra left. I look forward to the evenings when I have dates with you—but I dread them too. We talk. We make conversation. But with Myra at the back of your mind every second, it's an agony for me. I want no more of it. When Myra ran away I was happy, I thought—

there, I'm rid of her. But I'm not. She's here. I'm not rid of her. I'll never be rid of her. If I felt there was any future in Myra for you I'd—I'd—

WILLIE (*Comes close to her*) Leah—dearest Leah—

LEAH Don't come near me! I wish Myra were dead!

WILLIE (*Whispers to her*) Leah. Sweet Leah. I adore you. I love you. Darling Leah . . .

LEAH She doesn't love you—but I do. That's why she won't sleep with you, because she doesn't love you—but I love you, Willie . . .

(*He kisses her. The kiss becomes long and passionate*)

The Lights Dim Out

SCENE FOUR

Several days later.
The lights go up on MR. SACHER'S *room.* TOBEY *is curled up reading. From the next room we hear* MR. SACHER'S *nighttime prayer.*

MR. SACHER'S VOICE ". . . May the angel Michael be at my right hand, Gabriel at my left . . ."

TOBEY (*Looks up from his book, calls*) Father! Father!

FATHER (*Comes in*) Yes, Tobey. What is it?

TOBEY Those four angels you're always praying to—

FATHER Well?

TOBEY Why don't they *do* more?

FATHER They do the best they can!

TOBEY They couldn't save Mother. Is it because they're good that they can't do more?

FATHER The good are not without power, Tobey. Their very existence is a power. (*We see* WILLIE *coming up the street with his suitcase*) Otherwise the evil would have the field to themselves.

TOBEY   They certainly give those good angels a hard time! (WILLIE *reaches the stoop and whistles his Beethoven signal.* TOBEY *jumps up and goes to the door*)

FATHER   Here comes the oracle—turn over your questions to him.
(WILLIE *comes into the room*)

TOBEY   Hello, Willie. You going someplace?

WILLIE   New York.

TOBEY   When?

WILLIE   (*Puts suitcase down*)   Tonight. I know it's late, Mr. Sacher. I just had to say good-bye to Tobey.

FATHER   How long are you going for, Willie?

WILLIE   For good, I hope.

FATHER   What about your job here?

WILLIE   I'll get a better one in New York.

FATHER   Yes?

WILLIE   I've got plans for Tobey too. I know he wants to be a composer. When he gets through school I want him to join me in New York. That's where the opportunity is.

FATHER   Your plans are far-ranging, Willie. Now what made you reach this decision so suddenly?

WILLIE   It's not sudden. I've been planning this for some time.

FATHER   Myra?

WILLIE   I've had a telegram from her. She needs me.

FATHER   So this is your objective?

WILLIE   What's wrong with that?

FATHER   It isn't enough.

WILLIE   My other objectives are boundless.

FATHER   That's too much.

WILLIE   (*Teasing, with humor*)   Not for me. I'm insatiable. I'm going to cross all frontiers, master all the disciplines, then come back here and emancipate you.

FATHER   Oh, Willie, you won't be able to emancipate anybody until you've disciplined yourself.

WILLIE   (*In mock despair*)   I'm afraid my mission will fail. You live in a closed world.

FATHER   And you live in a limitless one.

WILLIE   It gives me more room.

FATHER You joke, but that is your danger—too much room. Because there must be limits—that's what sanity is—a sense of limitation.

WILLIE What are limits for you are chains for me.

FATHER Words. Words. Admit it, Willie—you're chasing Myra. She doesn't love you. She'll never love you. Why don't you declare a loss and turn to someone else?

WILLIE Because I'm afraid of bankruptcy. I can't expect you to understand what I feel for Myra. Myra's installed inside me, independent of me, feeding upon me, but it has nothing to do with Myra really.

FATHER Evidently you prefer mystery to light—the riddle to the answer. And all your gifts will go for nothing. (WILLIE *turns away*) I'm concerned about you, Willie. You run a grave risk.

WILLIE (*Turns back*) Life *is* a risk. Life *is* a danger. I'm not lucky the way you are—to be securely locked in a cell of faith. I wouldn't exchange my danger for all your security.

FATHER You wave your danger like a banner. The facts of life may be pedestrian, but they are unalterable. You charge at them, but they will resist your charge, and you will come out the loser . . . Good-bye, Willie . . .

WILLIE (*As he grabs his suitcase and runs out*) I'll write you, Tobey!
　　　　(*The lights dim down to come up on the stoop*)

Eli Wallach, Timmy Everett and Morris Carnovsky,
as WILLIE, TOBEY and MR. SACHER

TOBEY (*Following* WILLIE *to the stoop*) Willie! Willie! (WILLIE *stops*) Willie, you're terribly angry with Father, aren't you?

WILLIE Yes. I am.

TOBEY Why?

WILLIE Because he told the truth.

TOBEY Then why are you going?

WILLIE Because I must.

TOBEY I see you must.

WILLIE Whatever it is ahead of me I've got to meet it—I've got to meet it head on.

TOBEY Have you told Leah?

WILLIE Yes. It's too late now, Tobey. (*A moment. He consciously lightens the mood*) New York isn't Europe after all. You'll write. I'll write. We'll keep in touch. (*A pause. He reaches out his hand to* TOBEY. *They shake hands like two men*) So long, Tobey.

TOBEY (*Fighting tears*) So long, Willie.

WILLIE Work hard. Keep well.

TOBEY You too, Willie.

WILLIE (*Starts up the hill, stops*)   Finish *Opus One*.

TOBEY   I will. I'll finish it. (WILLIE *goes quickly*) Don't go, Willie. Don't go.

The Curtain Falls

ACT THREE

SCENE ONE

New York City, five years later. The set consists of IDA's *living room, stage right; and* TOBEY's *and* WILLIE's *garret-living room, stage left.*

IDA's *flat is directly across the hall from her father's on West Eighty-sixth Street. A few pieces from Providence Street have been moved here. Prominently placed is the imposing, large photograph of her father, the Ramov.*

The lights come up on TOBEY's *and* WILLIE's *flat, which is in Morningside Heights. On the easel of a cheap upright piano are* TOBEY's *music-manuscript papers. Nearby is a bridge table, with a green-shaded light over it, over which* TOBEY *is leaning, composing away. Every once in a while he experiments with a dissonant phrase on the piano, which he can do without moving from the table. He is in a profound concentration. The piece on which he is working is as far removed as possible in spirit from the melodious and pensive Chopin which we heard him play in Act Two. His own composition is jagged, dissonant, very modern.*

When the telephone rings, TOBEY *answers it. It is* IDA, *from the living room of her flat. As he reaches the phone and picks up the receiver, we light up on* IDA's *flat.*

TOBEY   Hello.

IDA (*On the telephone*)   Hello it's you, Tobey?

TOBEY   Yes. How are you, Ida?

IDA   Fine. But this is not why I called you. Willie is there?

TOBEY   Not just now. I know he has a date with Myra.

IDA   So why is he chasing with that Myra when she is crazy in love with another man?

TOBEY   That's a tough question to answer. I find it hard to pin Willie down these days—a bit like trying to put mist in a bottle.

IDA   But this is not why I called you. Why I called you is to tell you Leah is back from Chicago.

TOBEY   Oh, that's nice. How is she?

IDA   Wonderful. A wonderful job she has on Fourteenth Street. With me she is staying till she finds an apartment. The baby she adapted is here too. Wait till you see him, Tobey, you'll right away melt. What I want you should come to dinner and Willie he should come too.

TOBEY   *With* Myra?

IDA   Better without. But if I have to I have to. Leah is crazy to see you, Tobey, so come right away. Come quick.

TOBEY   O.K.
      (*She hangs up. We see* TOBEY *hang up. He is smiling. He picks up his manuscript, looks at it, throws it down with a kind of disgust—then he picks up his coat and starts out for* IDA'*s. The light dims down on* TOBEY'*s apartment.*

Just as IDA *leaves the telephone in her apartment it rings again.* IDA *turns to answer it*)

IDA (*On phone*) So who are you? . . . Oh, Mrs. Grodberg from Fourteen F . . . Tell me, Mrs. Grodberg, do I know you? . . . At my stepmother's funeral was the whole city of New York so I'm sorry I don't remember you, Mrs. Grodberg . . . To my father you want an introduction? . . . Tell me, Mrs. Grodberg, are you healthy? . . . (REN *comes in, now an attractive young miss. She listens to her mother with some impatience*) Are you pious? . . . I had in mind a Boston woman with whom my father could live out his life . . . well, promises I can't make, Mrs. Grodberg, but I will keep you in mind . . . Yes, yes, I will mention to Poppa . . . (*Kindly*) On pins and needles you shouldn't be sitting because a long time you may be sitting . . . So good-bye, Mrs. Grodberg. (IDA *hangs up. She looks at* REN, *overwhelmed by her responsibilities*) Till I find for Poppa I won't have a moment's peace!

REN Is Myra coming for dinner?

IDA Maybe. That hitzel-dritzel is always with a maybe.

REN (*Swooning over* MYRA) She's so *glamorous*. Wasn't she beautiful in the show?

IDA Beautiful she was, but so undressed I thought any minute they would turn the shower bath on her. What do you think, Ren? From Mandel I had a ring.

REN Congratulations! Are you engaged?

IDA On the telephone. He's coming.

REN You're so busy marrying off other people you don't notice anything about *me*. I am going through a crisis. I'm crazy about this boy I met, a French major at Columbia.

IDA So bring him.

REN He keeps putting me off. He prefers *common* girls.

IDA A Frenchman! What do you expect?

REN Oh, Ma, you're hopeless.

IDA Don't worry, darling, when the time comes for you I'll find.

REN The time is *now*, Ma!

IDA Now is the time I wish you would go in the kitchen and peel some onions.

REN (*With disdain*) Onions!
　　(*The doorbell rings.* IDA *gets up*)

IDA So here is Mandel.
　　(*She goes out to the hallway.* REN *looks at herself in the mirror, does something to her hair*)

REN (*Bitterly*) Onions!
　　(*But she yields to the exigencies of existence and goes into the kitchen.* IDA *comes in with* MANDEL. MANDEL *is tanned almost to blackness. He wears a sharkskin suit and twirls a cane*)

IDA (*Palpitating in spite of herself*) A joy it is to see you, Mandel!

MANDEL (*Very formal*) Did you receive my communication from Florida?

IDA I received but I did not answer because I was cool to you. Now I see you I tell you the truth my heart jumps. How can this be when I am cool? (MANDEL *twirls his ginger-colored mustache—does not deign to comment on this paradox.* IDA *stares at him with rapt admiration*) Tell me, Mandel. This color you are all over?

MANDEL (*With great delicacy*) With certain considerations, Mrs. Feinberg. I understand Miss Long is now back from Chicago and residing on these premises.

IDA She is.

MANDEL I told you years ago Norbert Mandel has great will-power. He never gives up.

IDA So what don't he give up?

MANDEL Leah from Fitchburg. That's what he don't give up.

IDA Leah put out of your mind.

MANDEL Norbert Mandel is faithful! Norbert Mandel is stead-fast! He don't switch!

IDA With Leah you don't fit, Mandel.
(*He walks away, swinging his cane debonairly. He abandons Romeo, becomes Machiavelli.* IDA *watches him, fascinated*)

MANDEL (*Twirling his cane in large circles*) While she was in Chicago I understand Leah took it into her head to adapt a baby.

IDA So what has that?

MANDEL A very peculiar thing, you will admit, for a young girl to do.
(LEAH *comes in. She is older, but very handsome, assured and smart*)

LEAH (*Breathless*) Oh, Ida, I'm so lucky. I've found a lovely apartment right—(*Sees* MANDEL) Oh, Mr. Mandel.

MANDEL (*All charm*) Why so formal? After the length of our acquaintanceship you are surely justified in calling me Norbert.

IDA (*Helping as far as she can*) Yes, Leah. Call him Norbert. You'll feel closer.

LEAH I've got quite a lot on my mind.

IDA So how long does it take to call him Norbert?

MANDEL (*To* LEAH) You are starting in, I understand, as buyer in a dress shop on Fourteenth Street.

LEAH Yes. I am.

MANDEL Should be with luck.

LEAH Thank you.

114

MANDEL   In Boston I have just acquired an important situation where I plan to put up a superior market.

LEAH   I'm glad. (*As she starts for the bedroom*) I'm afraid you'll have to excuse me. I want to look in on my baby.

MANDEL (*Flushes*)   Norbert Mandel is not used to being cut off in the middle. (*A moment. He glares*) Norbert Mandel is a busy man! (*Looks at his watch*) In a half-hour I have with a syndicate. (*He is simmering with fury. He moves to the door*) Norbert Mandel knows when he is not welcome. (*A moment; revengeful*) And how is your baby, Miss Long?

LEAH   Very well, thank you.

MANDEL   Norbert Mandel likes children, Miss Long. Maybe it is better for the baby you should the sooner the better be *Mrs.* Long.
(*At this* IDA's *eyes flash*)

IDA (*Rises*)   Mandel—what are you grabbling?

MANDEL   I think Miss Long knows.

IDA   Listen to me, Mandel! Cool I was to you already. Now I am frozen!

MANDEL (*Drops* IDA, *addresses* LEAH)   At your feet, Miss Long, Norbert Mandel lays his heart—baby or no baby. Should you care to communicate with me I am in Rooms Two thirty-four, Two thirty-five in the Waldorf-Astoria Hotel on Thirty-fourth Street and Fifth Avenue.

IDA (*In spite of herself this tidbit fascinates her*)   Two rooms you have, Mandel!

MANDEL   Yes. Norbert Mandel always takes two rooms. One is for sitting.

IDA   Mandel, you should not come here again. Go to your rooms and sit in both of them.

MANDEL (*Appeals to* IDA *with great sincerity*)   Mrs. Feinberg— tell her. What I feel for Miss Long is the kind of occurrence that occurs once in a lifetime. (*His voice rises*) I am en- amored. Deeply enamored.

IDA   You hear, Leah, what he is?

MANDEL   I want her to do me the honor to be my bride. (*He faces* LEAH. *He suddenly loses all his bravado. He has the courage, facing defeat, to reveal it as a façade*) Miss Long, I am not a refined man. But my heart is in the right place. Miss Long, with you I could become refined. With you I could become educated. Please, Miss Long.

LEAH (*Touched*)   I'm sorry, Norbert—I'm very sorry.

MANDEL   This is the last appeal of Norbert Mandel. What are you now? A buyer with an adapted baby that's not adapted. (*He goes out.* IDA's *eyes blaze. She turns to* LEAH)

IDA   That he should let a thing like that drop from his mouth— never again will I arrange for Mandel!

LEAH (*Quietly*)   It's true though, Ida.

IDA   To such slanders you shouldn't even listen!

LEAH (*Very moved by* IDA's *faith*)   But *I* am telling you, Ida.

116

IDA (*Overcome with shock*)   Oh, I forgot. You I have to believe.

LEAH   I lied to you five years ago about my reason for going to Chicago. I was afraid it would be a shock to you.

IDA   So how could it be a shock if you did it?

LEAH   I went there—and got a job there—to have my baby.

IDA (*Grasping at a straw*)   So it must be you're married?

LEAH   No, Ida, I'm not married.

IDA (*Still struggling with the horrendous fact*)   But, Leah treasure! If you had a baby—even if all by yourself—he must have a father! (*Looks up at her*) So who is the father?

LEAH   Willie Lavin.

IDA (*Gets up indignantly*)   Willie Lavin! This from Willie Lavin I wouldn't believe.

LEAH (*Smiles faintly*)   I had more to do with it than he did. Don't blame him! He was perfectly honest. He was always crazy about Myra. He never pretended.

IDA   But why didn't *he* tell me?

LEAH   Because he doesn't know. That's why I went to Chicago in the first place. Because I didn't want him to know.

IDA   He must right away marry you!

LEAH (*Very firm*)   He doesn't know and I don't want him to know and I trust you not to tell him.

IDA   But for the baby it's no good. Not to have even a father!

LEAH   I've been through all that. I had a terrible struggle about that. It's all I'll ever have of Willie's and I *wanted* it—because I wanted Willie.

IDA   (*Bewildered, it is too much for her*)   But, Leah angel, don't you *want* to get married?

LEAH   Not in the least.

IDA   (*Her universe overturned*)   A wonderful girl like you should be an old maid!

LEAH   (*Smiles*)   Well, not quite.

IDA   When you wrote me you adapted a baby, I said to myself, "How can you take in your house a perfect stranger?" Now I see he wasn't such a stranger!

LEAH   That's right—he's no stranger.

IDA   (*Moved*)   The poor little orphan.

LEAH   (*Laughs. Rises, starts toward bedroom*)   Not yet, Ida. I'm very much alive! (*Stops a moment at the door*) I can trust you, can't I? Not to tell *anybody*—nobody in the whole world.

IDA   Who should I tell? (*Thinks a moment*) I think I'll call up Mandel and invite him to dinner.

LEAH   What for?

118

IDA   Now that I know it's true what he said I want to tell him he's a liar.

LEAH *(Laughs)*   Oh, Ida!
     (She blows IDA a kiss and goes inside. IDA is in a daze. She sits, fans herself with the edge of her kitchen apron. REN comes in from the kitchen)

REN   I can't cope with any more onions, Ma. Let me arrange the flowers on the dining-room table.

IDA *(Sits, overcome by her worry. To get rid of REN—)*   Arrange! Arrange!

REN   What's the matter, Ma?

IDA   Everything! *(Catches herself)* I mean nothing. *(The telephone rings. IDA rises, goes and picks up the receiver)* Hello— the number you have right but the exchange is not right, so who are you?— It's too bad, Mr. Brown, you have a wrong number, but anyway call me later because now I'm busy. Glad to have met you, Mr. Brown.
     (She hangs up and sits on the chair)

REN   Ma! It was a wrong number! Why did you ask him to call back?

IDA   A nice voice he had, very educated, and he sounded lonely.

REN   Oh, Ma!
     (She goes out to the dining room as TOBEY comes in)

TOBEY   Hello, Ida.

IDA (*Absently, without looking at him, her mind awhirl*) Oh, come in Tobey life.
(*She rises*)

TOBEY (*Kisses her on the cheek*) How are you, Ida?

IDA This don't ask me.

TOBEY What's wrong?

IDA (*Sitting on sofa*) This don't ask me either.

TOBEY Anything serious?

IDA Tobey. To you I have to talk. To you I have to tell a secret. But first you must promise me—by your mother-may-she-rest-in-peace you must promise me—that what I'm telling you won't tell a living soul.

TOBEY (*Sits beside her*) I promise.

IDA You heard that in Chicago Leah adapted a baby?

TOBEY Yes. I did.

IDA *She didn't adapt*. She *had*.

TOBEY (*This is a surprise*) Are you sure?

IDA More sure I couldn't be! But I have your promise, Tobey—not to tell anybody in the whole world.

TOBEY (*Sincerely*) Of course you have!

120

IDA (*Abruptly*) Except Willie Lavin! Him you can tell!
(*As he looks at her, he rises slowly, comprehension of
the truth and of the meaning of her maneuver breaking
in on him*)

The Lights Dim Out

Scene Two

At TOBEY's. *The next evening.*

WILLIE *is pacing in their room.* TOBEY *comes in, taut with determination to make* WILLIE *live up to his responsibilities.*

WILLIE   Hello, Tobey.

TOBEY   I'm glad I found you. I want to talk to you. I waited up for you last night.

WILLIE   I was with Myra. But I've been waiting for you too, Tobey. I have something I want to speak to you about.

TOBEY   Look, Willie, sit down.

WILLIE   (*Cuts in, doesn't sit, picks up* TOBEY's *score*) How's it going? (TOBEY *makes a gesture of disgust at his manuscript*) Heard yet from that fellow you submitted your piece to?

TOBEY   George Slocum. I've been expecting a call all day but I haven't heard from him, probably never will. What the hell ever made me think I was a composer anyway? (*Sitting on piano stool*) But that's not what I want to talk to you about.

WILLIE   (*Cutting in again*)   Congratulate me. I passed my bar exams.

TOBEY   Congratulations. But I'm not surprised. You can do anything when you set your mind to it.

WILLIE   But, Tobey, I want to ask you a favor.

TOBEY   What?

WILLIE   I want to go back to Worcester. I want you to come with me.

TOBEY   What for?

WILLIE   Impulse to revisit the scenes of our youth. Think things over. Get back to first principles. I've come to a kind of conclusion, Tobey—it'll probably seem strange to you. I passed the bar exam with flying colors, but the thought of practicing law revolts me. Now for the first time I feel I know what I want to do.

TOBEY   Now listen to me, Willie.

WILLIE   (*Sitting on the bed*)   Here's the thing. I'm sick of the endless revolutions of my thoughts. I'm sick of pondering the mysteries that are insoluble. Everything is a question, everything is a dilemma. I long, Tobey, for the simple, the finite, the concrete.

TOBEY   That's wonderful. I'm happy to hear you say that, Willie. That's exactly what I want to talk to you about.

WILLIE   (*Presses on. Passes his hand over his forehead*)   I don't sleep, you know, Tobey. I want to forget everything I've ever studied, ever thought. I want to go back to Worcester—get a job.

TOBEY You better listen to me, Willie, before you fly off on another tangent.

WILLIE No. But this is sound. No tangent. I want to go back and take a job in a factory. I want to do a job that requires no thought, tending a machine. I want to be tired at the end of the day, Tobey—spent—so tired that I'll fall into dreamless sleep. Will you know me in overalls, Tobey?

TOBEY (*Deeply disturbed. A moment*) Willie . . . I've got to have your attention about something vital.

WILLIE Oh, by the way, Myra wants to have dinner with us.

TOBEY Hasn't she gone to California yet?

WILLIE That's all collapsed.

TOBEY Really?

WILLIE She doesn't project, it seems. That director she's in love with isn't taking her. All her hopes have vanished . . . to such a degree that she wants to marry me.

TOBEY (*Thinks he sees it now*) Will Myra consent to be the wife of a factory hand? I can't quite see her in that role.

WILLIE If I married her now it would be out of pity and she deserves better than that. The truth is I don't want to marry Myra.

TOBEY I don't believe that.

WILLIE Myra doesn't either. You know, Tobey, I've lived so long with this obsession for Myra that without it—I'd feel—unemployed.

TOBEY Willie, now for God's sake listen to me. If you really want the finite, the concrete, you don't have to go to a factory in Worcester. Because they're all right here for you.

WILLIE How?

TOBEY You have a responsibility here—to Leah.

WILLIE How can you trace responsibility to its ultimate source?

TOBEY (*Rises*) God damn it! Why do you talk about ultimate responsibility when you have an immediate one? Leah's adopted child is your child.

WILLIE (*After a moment*) That possibility has occurred to me, you know.

TOBEY It has?

WILLIE But I preferred to accept Leah's fiction.

TOBEY Well, now you know it isn't fiction. It's a fact. A fact which you must face.

WILLIE (*Suddenly docile, goes dead*) Tobey—the True Name of the Lord your father used to forbid you to seek. Do you remember?

TOBEY Yes. But what has that got to do with what we're talking about?

WILLIE (*Sitting on bed*) I used to think there was only one mystery, the key to everything, and you'd get it all in one blinding flash—

TOBEY Willie—please—

WILLIE (*In a spiral of amused speculation*) No, Tobey, no, it's just an amusing idea I had—a vagrant idea— It just occurs to me—the heart of the mystery, the mystery that is the core of everything—supposing by some lucky chance I did hit on it— probed it—supposing it turned out, this terrible secret, to be quite simple really—even a bore? (TOBEY *is staring at him in desperation, in agony, in despair*) I think that's funny. I thought it would amuse you. I see it doesn't.

TOBEY (*Sitting on the stool*) No, it doesn't amuse me.

WILLIE What were you saying, Tobey, what were you telling me?

TOBEY I was telling you about Leah.

WILLIE I think about Leah—the suffering she must have gone through.

TOBEY (*Jumps up, cutting him off*) Listen, Willie. I owe you more than I can ever possibly repay: you made me see life as a wonder and as an adventure. I owe you everything—even the truth. And the truth is that you have wasted yourself— scattered your gifts, as my father warned you. I remember your arguments with my father. He was right—all the way. You feel this need for the concrete, so you turn to manual labor, which will probably bore you to death after one week.

Another horizon, another mirage, another postponement. Chemistry. Law. What you know, what you have, you turn your back on. It is the unknowable that lures you. Even my talent is an unknown quantity and you made a concept out of that. Willie, the near things, the achievable things, the warm winds of affection, of friendship, of love, don't seem to touch you any more.

(*A pause*)

WILLIE You're right. I'm destructive to people—Leah—even Myra. I waited for Dan to die. He was my friend. When he died I couldn't repress a feeling of exaltation. Ethically speaking, I am a murderer.

TOBEY Concepts again! That's distortion. (*Sitting beside him*) Willie, for pity's sake, live your own life in *this* world. Attach yourself to something definite—with all the problems that go with it—Leah—your child—you could do for him what you've done for me.

WILLIE You're right about everything. The pupil has outstripped the master. In the kid is wisdom. Tell me what to do, Tobey, and I'll do it.

TOBEY I don't have to tell you. You know what to do.

WILLIE I'll go to Leah and ask her to marry me. (*A pause*) But what about Myra? She's coming here.

TOBEY (*Rises*) I'll take care of Myra. I'll take her to dinner.

WILLIE Call me from the restaurant.

TOBEY But you'll be proposing to Leah.

WILLIE (*Rises*) Then call me.

TOBEY What for?

WILLIE Just call me.

TOBEY If you like.

WILLIE I'll be waiting for your call.
>   (WILLIE *goes.* TOBEY *stares after him. He is deeply
>   troubled, quite uncertain whether he has had a victory.
>   He begins to pace the room, in unconcious imitation of
>   his father—his hands behind his back. Out of a deep
>   well of memory he begins to pray—as his father used to
>   pray*)

TOBEY "At my right the angel Michael, at my left Gabriel, and
over my head the Divine Presence of God . . ."

The Lights Dim Out

Scene Three

At IDA'S. *The action follows the preceding scene at* WILLIE'S. *The doorbell rings.* LEAH *goes to open it, admitting* WILLIE.

LEAH (*Very surprised, even a bit aghast. They stand face to face for a moment*)   Willie! Did you come to see me or Ida?

WILLIE   I came to see you.

LEAH (*Doesn't believe it*)   Well, Ida's gone out.

WILLIE (*After an awkward pause*)   Felt like seeing you.

LEAH   Well—thank you.
       (*Another awkward pause*)

WILLIE (*Points to her dress*)   Pretty dress, Leah.

LEAH   Oh, it's just a little number I picked off my own racks on Fourteenth Street. (*A moment*) Like a drink?

WILLIE   No, thanks.
       (*Another pause*)

LEAH   Well—sit down—relax. Working for the bar exams, I hear.

WILLIE Just passed them. (*A moment. She looks at him; she is mystified by his visit. He starts walking around the room, suddenly wheels around, shoots the question at her*) How would you like to be a lawyer's wife, Leah?

LEAH (*A moment, lightly*) Are you proposing to me?

WILLIE (*Meets her look*) Yes.

LEAH (*It flashes through her mind that he has heard about the paternity of the baby*) Why?

WILLIE I've been thinking about you—and I want to.

LEAH What about Myra?

WILLIE Myra's out of my life.

LEAH (*Smiles at him*) Is *that* why you're proposing to me? Is Myra getting married?

WILLIE Not as far as I know.

LEAH Anyway—do have a drink.

WILLIE Anything—(LEAH *moves at once to the little bar, fixes two drinks and hands one to him.* WILLIE *takes the drink and lifts the glass in a toast to her*) Cheers!

LEAH (*Touches her glass to his*) Cheers!

WILLIE To our future. (*She laughs*) What's the joke?

LEAH What a funny man you are!

130

WILLIE (*Bleakly. Puts his glass down on bar*) I can be funny on occasion.
(*A moment. She keeps studying him*)

LEAH You know, I suppose, that I've adopted a baby.

WILLIE Yes. Ida told me.

LEAH (*Points to bedroom*) He's asleep. In there. Would you like a look at him?

WILLIE No thanks.

LEAH I know! Other people's babies are always a bore.

WILLIE But you haven't answered my question.

LEAH What?

WILLIE How you would like to be a lawyer's wife.

LEAH And you haven't answered mine.

WILLIE What was that?

LEAH About Myra. She's probably walking out on you again. So you come in here and ask me to marry you. (*Moves away from him*) Well, I won't. I don't want to marry you. Nor anybody.

WILLIE It seems unfair to yourself.

LEAH You must understand my position.

WILLIE I understand. You don't love me any more.

LEAH (*In a low voice*)   I do though. I'll never love anybody else.

WILLIE   Then why? . . .

LEAH   I couldn't marry you because I don't think I could stand the perpetual threat of Myra.

WILLIE (*With anger*)   It's all over—I've told you—between Myra and me. Over!

LEAH   I'd hate to put you to the test!

WILLIE (*His voice rises*)   THEN STOP DOING IT! I've just been telling Tobey—Myra means nothing to me!

LEAH   I wonder.

WILLIE (*Begins to lose control of himself*)   I BEG YOU, LEAH—DON'T CROSS EXAMINE ME.

LEAH (*Going to him. Relentless*)   Perhaps Ida told you something more. (*She waits. He says nothing. He sits on the hassock*) I asked her not to. (*He is still silent.* LEAH *knows now*) So that's why you're here! To make an honest woman out of me! Good, moral boy from Worcester!

WILLIE (*In manic fury*)   You drive me crazy. Stop analyzing. I want you to marry me. I have the right to marry you. CAN'T YOU JUST ACCEPT THE FACT? I love you. I admire you. (*Rises*) Isn't that enough for you? Have a heart, Leah! Give me a chance, can't you! (*Sitting on sofa*) You don't risk anything.

LEAH (*Turns to him. Her voice rises*) I risk this hold Myra has over you!

WILLIE Don't keep flinging Myra at me. It's broken I tell you. How many times do I have to tell you? There's no hope in Myra—not only for me—for anybody. Nor for herself. Shall I tell you why? She's in pursuit of a romantic ideal. She'll pursue it endlessly. It will elude her endlessly.

LEAH (*Beginning to be persuaded*) It's taken you a long time to find this out about Myra.

WILLIE No. I always knew it.

LEAH (*Passionately*) Then why, Willie . . . why have you let it drag on so long?

WILLIE (*Quiets down, very clever, aware that he is pouring the word into an ear less subtle than his own*) What I have felt for Myra was an obsession. Nothing more. What I feel for you—what I have always felt for you—is real.
(*This does it. This persuades her. She goes to him, overcome with compassion and love for him*)

LEAH (*Kneeling beside him*) Willie! Willie! (*She embraces him. A silence. Quietly—*) In my heart I have always been married to you. Don't you know that?

WILLIE (*Numbly*) It's all right, darling. (*With a little laugh*) I accept you. I hadn't realized it was possible.

LEAH What?

WILLIE It's odd, with you I feel peace—security—a kind of peace.

(There is a long silence. She kneels beside him, holding his hand on the arm of the sofa)

LEAH *(Very moved)* I can hardly believe it—I can hardly—oh, Willie, Willie, Willie—after all we've been through!

WILLIE It's settled, isn't it, Leah, between us, the two of us—we're committed to each other, aren't we?

(The outside door is heard closing. IDA comes in)

IDA Did I stay away long enough?

LEAH *(Gets up, smiles at her)* Yes, you did, Ida. Just long enough.

WILLIE There's no doubt about it, Ida—when you die, there will be joy in Heaven among all the unmarried angels.

IDA *(Hugging LEAH)* What I want there should be joy on *earth* among all the unmarried angels. *(Hugs WILLIE)* With you, Willie, such a slow poke you are I began to give up hope.

WILLIE *(Infuriated with his own bravura. Sits on sofa)* Slow poke. Admitted. But you, Ida, you marry people off by instinct. You rush them to the altar. You seem unaware of the immense responsibility. For a girl like Leah the alternatives are endless. How can you settle on me? Think of it, Ida—consummation! *(He rises)* "For as long as you both shall live." For eternity! That's a long time, darling. Who knows what lurks in the distance—for Leah? For me? What angers, what bitterness, accidents, disaster, deathknell sounding through the wedding bells!

IDA   Wedding bells you and Leah don't need. They'll wake up
the baby! (*To* LEAH) You told him yet that he's going to have
a father?

LEAH   I'll wake him up now to break the news to him. (LEAH
starts out; WILLIE *starts to follow. She stops at the door, kisses*
WILLIE, *faces him toward* IDA) I'll tell it to him gently.
    (*She goes*)

IDA   Willie darling, so long I waited to see this day I thought it
would never come.

WILLIE (*After a pause*)   Perhaps it's come too late, darling.

IDA   What too late?

WILLIE   Too late for the near horizons—I abdicate!

IDA   What are you talking?

WILLIE (*His exuberance gone—tender, and with abdication*)
    Ida. Ida. Ida.
        (*He sinks into the sofa*)

IDA (*Rises, going to him*)   Willie! Willie!
        (*The telephone rings*)

WILLIE   That's Tobey.

IDA (*Rises*)   So ask him to come over—so we can tell the good
news—
        (*By this time* WILLIE *is on the phone*)

WILLIE Tobey . . . where are you? At the restaurant? You got your call from Slocum—he's going to play it! Oh, Tobey, that's great! I'll meet you at the apartment . . . I'll tell you later, Tobey . . . Good-bye, Tobey. (*He hangs up. Goes to* IDA) Tobey's having his first performance. Isn't that wonderful! I feel as happy about this as you do, Ida, when you pull off a match. It's a funny thing, Ida, that the only responsibility I have ever recognized is my responsibility to Tobey. He's grown-up—surpassed me, as I knew he would. But my faith in Tobey and what he might do . . . that was tangible— that was real—and not as Tobey thinks—a concept . . . Good-bye . . . I love you—
> (*He starts out*)

IDA What are you rushing?

WILLIE (*Comes back*) I want you to give Tobey a message for me.

IDA But I just heard you—you're going to see Tobey.

WILLIE In case I miss him, Ida—in case I miss him—

IDA So what should I tell him? (*He stands silent, as if he hadn't heard her. To rouse him out of his trance, frightened—*) Willie life—look at me—what should I tell Tobey?

WILLIE Tell him!

IDA So?

WILLIE Tell him he's right about the factory in Worcester— instead tell him I'm going to stop holding on to the bedposts. Can you remember that? Good-bye. I love you.
> (*He rushes out*)

IDA Willie! Willie! (IDA *starts for the bedroom, then runs to the telephone*) Central, get me Schuyler nine-seven-four. (*The lights come up in* TOBEY'S *apartment.* TOBEY *comes into his room as the telephone rings*)

TOBEY (*Sitting on bed, picks up the receiver*) Hello.

IDA Hello, Tobey.

TOBEY Ida, where's Willie? I can't wait to talk to him about my concert!

IDA Tobey, from Willie I'm worried—all settled he is with Leah and all of a sudden—

TOBEY What?

IDA You he runs to see.

TOBEY That's all right. We arranged it that way—

IDA All right it isn't.

TOBEY Why?

IDA He said good-bye to me as if he was saying good-bye . . . Go down stairs to the sidewalk—wait for him, Tobey—grab him, Tobey!

TOBEY All right.

IDA Something else he told me to tell you, Tobey. Crazy it sounded— He said I should tell you that no longer he's holding on to the bedposts. (TOBEY's *hand holding the receiver goes limp. It falls to his lap*) What does he mean? Tobey ... (*As she gets no answer she jiggles the phone in terror*) Tobey! Tobey! Tobey!

The Lights Dim Out

Scene Four

Back in Worcester. The street leading to JIM's *office. We hear the oboe:* JIM *is playing the melody from Handel's* Water Music, *as at the beginning of the play.*

Summer twilight. TOBEY *is walking to* JIM's *office—as we saw him with* WILLIE *when he was a child.* TOBEY's *walk is slow, dejected. He pushes the bell button.*

We light up on JIM's *office, unchanged, and see* JIM *putting down his oboe, as we saw him do earlier when he admitted* TOBEY *and* WILLIE.

JIM   Well, Tobey! I've been expecting you! How are you?
(*They shake hands*)

TOBEY   Just about as low as you can get. Felt I had to come back here. I wanted to revisit the scenes where Willie and I were happy—when we didn't know what was ahead of us—doom for Willie—despair for me.

JIM   Now, Tobey! Tobey, pessimism is easy. Despair is a luxury you can't afford. Sit down.
(*He points to the sofa*)

TOBEY   Same old sofa.

JIM   Naturally.

TOBEY   Still a symbol of conquest?

JIM   Alas, only a symbol. The sofa is willing, but the flesh is weak.

TOBEY   Jim—
    (*He sits on the sofa*)

JIM (*Sitting beside him*)   Yes, Tobey.

TOBEY   Willie—(*But he can't. His head sinks in his hands and he shakes it in misery*) No use. I can't.

JIM   Look, Tobey. You could have done nothing for Willie, I assure you.

TOBEY   He asked me to come here with him. Maybe if I had come—

JIM   It would have done no good. Willie was without an anchor—the anchor of reality. He couldn't face the everyday responsibilities of a permanent attachment—not only to a woman but to a job.

TOBEY (*With bitter self-reproach*)   And yet—the last time I saw him—I pushed him into reality.

JIM   It had nothing to do with you. Suicide, you know, is self-criticism in its most acute form.

TOBEY (*Gets up, starts to walk the room, flailing in self-abasement*)   The worst of it is—do you know why I didn't come with him when he asked me?

JIM   Why?

TOBEY   Because I was all excited over the performance of a piece I'd written.

JIM   How did it go, the concert?

TOBEY   Disaster.

JIM   Didn't anybody care for it.

TOBEY   A few fanatics for modern music like myself. One critic—

JIM (*Rises*)   Wonderful! One whole critic!

TOBEY   You should have seen the others! I am a failure as an artist. A failure as a friend.

JIM   You can't be a failure at your age. It takes much longer to achieve solid failure. You're lucky to get your first failure over with so early. The sooner to get to your second!

TOBEY   But this is it, Jim—half the time it's not Willie I'm thinking of, it's that damned concert! (*Summing it up*) Look, Jim—it is a world without Willie, and still the ego twitches.

JIM   Thank God. Once the ego stops twitching not even a great doctor like myself can do anything! What are you doing for dinner?

TOBEY   I'm free.

JIM Come back at eight and I'll take you to Putnam and Thurston's.

TOBEY (*Rises, starts out; stops*) Jim, now that I'm back here, the whole past is like a heavy sack around me. All the dead— my father and mother—Dan and Willie—the anonymous dead. (*Sits on sofa*) What does it all mean anyway?

JIM Why does life have to have meaning? It's good in itself. That oboe is good. What Willie gave you was good. Dinner tonight will be good—I hope! (*Sitting beside him*) You speak of the anonymous dead. They're not anonymous. They're figures in the tapestry in which we ourselves are figures. They've given us what we are. When you're young, you try to get away from them. But when you're mature, you return to them. You'll embrace them. And they'll support you, I promise you. Every breath you draw—every thought you have— every note you set down—you're living off them. (*Rises*) Now, clear out!

TOBEY (*Rises, goes to door*) All right, Jim. I'll go. (*Stands at the door, looking out through the twilight*) The seven hills of Worcester . . .

JIM (*Brusquely*) Lift your eyes to them! See you at eight!
     (TOBEY *goes out.* JIM *starts playing his oboe. We see* TOBEY, *his stance more buoyant, his head up, walking down the street accompanied by the sound of Handel's melody*)

The Curtain Falls